Yachting Wo

Other titles in the Adlard Coles Nautical humour series

Anchor's Aweigh
Des Sleightholme
ISBN 0-7136-4812-0
In his usual hilarious tongue-in-cheek manner, Des
Sleightholme introduces the newcomer to the joys of cruising.

'Des Sleightholme is one of the very few genuinely funny
yachting writers.' Andrew Bray, *Yachting World*

Off Watch with Old Harry
Des Sleightholme
ISBN 0-7136-4828-7
The 'joys' of antifouling, the bloody-mindedness of marine
engines, the dubious pleasures of sailing on a spring tide,
launchings and novice crew are just some of the subjects
aired by 'Old Harry'.

Old Harry's Dog-Watch
Des Sleightholme
ISBN 0-7136-4508-3
Perceptive, amusing and presented in his inimitable style,
Des Sleightholme takes us through further nautical hair-rais-
ing experiences. An ideal bunkside read.

Right to the Bitter End
Hilary Harron
ISBN 0-7136-4200-9
Hilary Harron takes the lid off the locker to expose all the
hidden tensions of sailing and provides hilarious advice to
help women put up with the men who sail with them.

Involuntary Jibes
Hilary Harron
ISBN 0-7136-4836-8
Why is sailing so stressful? If only we could learn to relax
and enjoy it. With this book the reader will learn how to give
their boat a 'makeover' so it feels just like a home-from-
home.

Yachting World's Dogwatch

John Passmore

Adlard Coles Nautical
LONDON

Published 1999 by Adlard Coles Nautical
an imprint of A & C Black (Publishers) Ltd
35 Bedford Row, London WC1R 4JH

ISBN 0-7136-5041-0

A CIP catalogue record for this book is available from the
British Library.

Typeset in 10.5 on 12 pt Palatino.
Printed and bound in Great Britain by Cromwell Press Ltd,
Trowbridge, Wiltshire

Dedication

This book is for my father George Passmore, who taught me to sail.

He also taught himself to sail. When he was seventeen he bought an 18 footer called *Wanderer* from Eric Hiscock. Years later they met at the Boat Show and Hiscock recalled, 'Ah yes, a pig of a boat, wasn't she?' *Wanderer* came with a ten foot clinker dinghy. In anything of a following sea this would try to climb into the cockpit. Father used to keep it at bay with the deck brush.

Over the years he has contributed quite a lot to *Dogwatch* and it is time to say thank you.

Contents

Introduction

Once in a while – once in a lifetime, perhaps – everyone gets offered the perfect job. Certainly that was what I thought when *Yachting World* wanted me to write each month about anything I liked, providing it had something to do with sailing and the accent was on humour. At that stage I had been writing for a living for more than 20 years and nobody had ever been so free with a brief before. Newspaper editors are notorious for having the most exact requirements – and then changing them along the way.

But, suddenly, here I was with the original carte blanche. It was like the childhood toy shop dream coming true. They even paid me. And, better still, the new commission coincided with the greatest upheaval of my sailing career. Until that time I had been mostly singlehanded, taking part in races like the OSTAR and Azores and Back, and telling people I did it for the company – it had to be for the company since *Largo* was a Rival 32 and considered five knots perfectly adequate.

At almost exactly the moment I started to write *Dogwatch*, I was swept away with the notion to give up the proper job and adopt the cruising life. Out of nowhere, there had appeared the ideal companion: Tamsin Rawlins is not only beautiful and enthusiastic but has never yet tied a bad knot, which is more than can be said for me.

And so the new column was timely for two reasons: it would provide a steady (if modest) income to help support us in our new life, and the life itself would provide an endless source of copy.

It was inevitable, therefore, that *Dogwatch* should develop as a diary of the liveaboard life, from the agony of selling the old boat, the fresh agonies of finding the new one and the sheer nightmare of trying to fit a complete existence into what turned out to be a 21 ft waterline.

As if this was not difficult enough, we were setting off not for the tropics but to go and inspect the rest of Britain. The reasoning seemed logical at the time: if we started with the palm trees, we were never going to get round to North Wales in January. And so the story unfolded through various layers of exasperation as we came to terms with the mud, the damp and the full majestic array of Britain's yacht club showers.

Then there was the dog. Tamsin had a dog. His name was Blue and he took to the sea with the sort of noble resignation that comes from an early life spent in a dog's home.

As a sort of distraction, we had a baby. He joined us in Wales and we called him Owen. He took to the sea with something approaching gusto and distinguished himself by being the only one who wasn't sick on the Irish Sea crossing. Now he is having to get used to sharing his cabin with his little brother Theo. A lot seems to have happened in five years.

This collection is the pick of it – the excitement and the embarrassment – and, somewhere in the midst of all that, there may even be some small lesson for anyone contemplating a similar great leap into a gentler lifestyle.

At the very least there should be the comfort of knowing that you are not alone in being quite unable to explain to your land-based friends just why it is that you have still not sailed round the world.

Two's Company

After a while, the singlehanded racing yachtsman gets a bit of a reputation. It's all to do with having a number painted on the hull and an Aries hanging off the stern; people think the skipper must be something of a hero.

This never worried me greatly. I might not be a Chichester or a Knox-Johnston but I can wax fairly lyrical on the subject of sleep deprivation off the Grand Banks or clocking 1,200 miles in nine days to come second in class in the Azores and Back (I have the engraved decanter to prove it).

But when someone looked down from the quay in Weymouth last summer, took in the name on the stern and shouted, 'Oi, aren't you supposed to be singlehanded?' it seemed that things had gone too far.

Tamsin was understandably miffed. She was, at the time, engaged in her role as one of the local sights – perched in the cockpit and plying the handle of our patent manual washing machine, a device which would not look out of place in an agricultural museum. But then she had never understood the attractions of singlehanded sailing, not least when I tried to explain the delights of being able to take meals straight from the saucepan without anyone complaining.

Of course there is more to it than that. Certainly there are moments when sailing alone over long distances can elevate a certain type of person to that state of supreme contentment which even pop stars, with all their pharmaceuticals, rarely manage to attain. But, at the same time, it does have its drawbacks.

I well remember my first long solo trip, from Poole to Northern Spain: by the time I got there, I was so bursting with pride I could hardly wait to tell someone – anyone. In the end I was reduced to going ashore for a solitary dinner and hoping for a chatty waitress (I didn't get one). But that is now part of a different and former existence. Now is the time to celebrate the pleasures of not being singlehanded. These, I should add, do *not* include sharing your life with a row of gorillas, whose idea of companionship is four hours jammed together on the weather rail, and who learned their personal hygiene in the rugby club changing room. Nor do I suggest getting up in the middle of the night to join one of those floating cocktail parties which move from marina to marina and measure the success of the cruise by the volume of the laughter in the cockpit at 0100.

No, this is about the backbone of the sailing fraternity – the cruising couple.

It would be unworthy, somehow, to start without recalling the magnificent teamwork involved in extracting the conduit from *Largo*'s mast without breaking it, demolishing anything particularly expensive or ending up on the sofa at Relate. Similarly, I see nothing sexist in appreciating the company of someone who can not only distinguish the leading marks as dusk falls on one of those tortuous Brittany rivers but who then, when the banks close in comfortingly from the murk, asks brightly, 'All right if I go and cook now?'

As a couple, you can invite the people on the next boat over for a drink, and find that they no longer hesitate as if wondering whether you might be desperate for someone to talk to and intend to pin them behind one warm beer for the rest of the day and lecture them into a state of coma. And, come the evening, the pair of you can sit in the cockpit in companionable silence and watch the comings and goings in the anchorage while making bets on how many times the new arrival, foredeck packed with wildly gesticulating crew, will circle before picking exactly the wrong spot.

Seasoned couples do not do things like that. Neither, ideally, do they make the evening echo to a duet of, 'Darling, for God's sake get it round something... Darling, I'm trying to. If only you wouldn't go so fast, Darling.'

Instead, the theory is that the sailing couple develop a rapport which has as much to do with togetherness as boat handling and which means that, but for the occasional dis-creet gesture, the manoeuvre is performed ostensibly by telepathy.

And then, when all is secure and the first noisy party from the next trot sets off for the pub, they can wrap a bottle of wine in a wet towel, climb into the dinghy and drift very gently up the river on the tide.

Two's Company

The first time we did this was on the Beaulieu River in Hampshire. We went so slowly that the ducks overtook us. When we finally rounded the bend into that hidden pool intended for bilge-keelers and poets, we found an elderly Westerly anchored there with a solitary figure in the cockpit, glass in hand, face tilted to the evening sun.

He opened his eyes, looked over the side and, in a conversational tone which carried in the stillness, remarked, 'You look happy.' And he was right.

Bumps in the Night

We called them the Colonel and his Lady. They were probably nothing of the kind but he stood ramrod straight and she seemed to be permanently on the point of offering sherry.

They were ensconced in Plouman'ach and appeared to have been there for some time. They had a 'gentleman's motor yacht' – no chrome or tinted glass but two thumping great diesels and all the right flags.

We were just about to come alongside and wondering how to scale the cliff-like bulwarks when the Colonel popped his head out of the wheelhouse, bursting with apologies, and suggested we try his other side, 'Feller who was here last night – nice chap – about your size – found it a bit shallow – try the other side – my advice...'

And so we did. They took our lines and chatted amiably. They were living aboard for the summer, something they had always planned to do although, as she said, 'You finally manage it and then you die; that's the awful thing.'

Not just then, of course. Instead she politely bustled off and left us to ourselves. A delightful couple, we decided, and so helpful. They quite made us review our prejudices about people with motorboats.

We were still thinking along these lines – if we thought anything at all – when, at about two in the morning, a roll of Sellotape fell off the chart table. Odd, that; it was calm in the entirely protected harbour. In fact it was very calm indeed, so calm that the boat seemed to have acquired a curious sort of solidity, almost as if she were a part of the land rather than the sea.

I rolled over to go back to sleep. It was very easy to roll over. In fact I had just reached that comfortable state of semi-consciousness when everything else fell off the chart table in an extended, if slightly hesitant, avalanche. Two pencils, the almanac, a bag of plums and Jilly Cooper's latest bonkbuster hit the floor one after the other with a sort of languorous crescendo that defied sleep.

4

Bumps in the Night

It was Tamsin whose mind managed to grasp the explanation first, 'We're aground,' she said.

At least that was what she tried to say. With the pair of us piled in a heap against the lockers, speech was a muffled business. I scrambled out and looked; the moon glistened on large expanses of mud and weed. The warps groaned.

Somewhere in my mind there danced the vision of cleats popping out of the deck like champagne corks, or possibly the motor yacht sedately toppling over and crushing us. I began to scuttle about the deck stark naked, easing things.

The clinometer on the compass pushed past 20 degrees, and then 30. Down below, the lockers became the berth. Tamsin crawled around the side of the boat, rearranging her bed through a right angle. There was another creak, another round of easing warps. I was running out of rope – 40 degrees.

The bilge water crept out from under the cabin sole and met the clothes which had slipped quietly off the settee berth. Things fell out of racks separately and at two-minute intervals. It was like living with a very lazy poltergeist.

I fished the almanac out of the soggy pile under the galley and looked up the tide tables. This was going to go on for another hour. It would be another three before we came remotely upright again.

For want of anything else to think about, I decided that we had grounded on a hump. Gradually the hump grew in detail, and the boat up-ended on it. If real life went the way of the nightmare then eventually the mast would dip below the horizontal. When the tide rose again *Largo* would fill with water as surely as a watering can dipped into a garden pond. I could see us climbing up the warps to save ourselves.

Going on deck was like working in a state of permanent broach. Amidships the toe-rail was under water. I poked about with an oar and found the bottom. At least it was there. We would not be going any further.

And sure enough, somewhere around four in the morning, *Largo* began to come up again. The dawn arrived, silhouetting Plouman'ach's peculiar rock formations against the grey in the east. The crew's spirits began to lift as well. After all there was nothing more to be done. The springs – living up to their name – would settle us back in position. It was time to get some sleep.

A good deal of thought went into this and a certain amount of trial and error. We ended up head to tail. Like sardines in a heavy and unromantic embrace, we lay there and listened while our world slowly rolled back into place again.

By breakfast time things looked surprisingly normal. The harbour was full of water once more, the muddy stain on *Largo*'s topsides was drying to a crust and, as on every other day of his life, the Colonel came to his door and sniffed the air. Then he asked pleasantly, 'Comfortable night?'

Tacking the Dog

The boat dog put his paws up on the gunwale and sniffed the salt air appreciatively. This is what he had been waiting for. This is what *we* had been waiting for. Ever since I introduced Blue, wrapped in a towel and being swayed aboard like Hornblower's cattle, this black labrador-cross, of such doubtful parentage that the term 'mongrel' is a positive compliment, has achieved an alarming celebrity status.

'So this is the famous boat dog,' people said as they found him sniffing his way round the boatyard when *Largo* came out for her scrub.

When we bought him a lifejacket, he swaggered around the pontoons as if he were modelling Armani instead of Crewsaver. Maybe he would turn out to be a born boat dog.

They can be found. I once knew one who could climb ladders – although going down again was a matter of his master standing in the dinghy, holding open his long and ancient oilskin coat. The dog would then launch himself from the quay and the two of them would land in a heap on the bottom boards.

We took Blue for a Sunday sail to see how he measured up. You might have thought the fuss in the Solent was all for him rather than the returning BT Challenge fleet. As we slipped out of Portsmouth harbour on a gentle reach, he sat there on the windward deck with his tongue out, positively basking in all the attention as everyone we passed smiled and exclaimed and pointed.

And then, with the world-weary air of one who has seen it all and forgotten most of it, the boat dog languorously crossed his front legs, laid his nose on top of them and went to sleep. Surreptitiously, we opened the ham salad rolls and toasted his success with last year's Kronenbourg.

At this point anyone who knows anything about boats – or indeed anything about dogs – could forgive themselves for muttering something about 'a false sense of security'. And very rightly too – because eventually we were going to have to turn round.

It happened midway between wondering where the massed fleet of spectator boats had got to and peering through binoculars at four irritatingly identical masts side by side in Ocean Village Marina. Sure enough, half the fleet had found the tidal gates up the Channel wide open for them and the other half were still being all high-minded and philosophical off St Alban's Head and would not be in before nightfall. So we gybed and began the long beat back against the tide.

And that was how we learned to tack the dog.

This is not a manoeuvre you will find in the sailing manuals but, after a good deal of trial and error, I suggest the most efficient system goes like this:

1 Depth recorder reading 2.5 m: look around, mainsheet traveller to leeward, dog to the cockpit.

2 Ready about: ease the sheet, dog's front feet to leeward seat.

3 Lee-ho: dog's front feet to side deck. Back feet to cockpit seat. Let fly the sheet.

4 Yacht settles on new tack: furious winching. Dog wanders up side deck, settles against coachroof. Crew grunt over last turn of winch. Dog yawns.

Of course it does not always happen like this. There is, for instance, the variation of: (a) Dog's tail laid across mainsheet track. (b) Dog puts all four feet in coils of headsail sheet. (c) Dog gets three feet out of cockpit and then tries to get back in again.

But, generally speaking, it went well enough – at least it did until the ferry went past.

Now, *Largo*, being a Rival, is a dry boat. She does not take much water on deck. However, she must have hit the ferry's wash awkwardly because a dollop of Solent came aboard and landed with astonishing accuracy right on top of the dozing dog. Not having the slightest idea where it had come from, he did what any sensible dog would do and retreated although, since he happened to be facing aft, that meant backing up towards the bow.

The second wave caught him right in his dignity. He stood there dripping and quivery and gave us the kind of look that suggested he had gone off the whole idea, that we were heartless and cruel and as soon as he got ashore he would ring Dogline and set Esther Rantzen on us. And we could hardly blame him.

On the other hand, once he had dried out and discovered all that salt to be licked off, he was back up there looking for all the world as if he had lived his life afloat. All we need, really, is a bigger boat; a boat, for instance, with a cockpit large enough for four pairs of feet and a tail.

One Careful Owner

The buyer stood in the cabin and made his offer. He made it hurriedly and rather loudly because, just at that moment, the prospective buyer started banging on the hull with his fist.

Anyone who ever tried to sell a boat should experience something like this once in their lives; it feels wonderful. The only trouble is that it does lead to a certain amount of embarrassment.

My problem was that, just as I accepted the offer, the prospective buyer started climbing the ladder: the three of us ended up in the cockpit simultaneously, and I had to do the explaining.

There are people, I suppose – the sort of people who buy and sell boats with the regularity of sock-changing – who find all this perfectly normal. But for those of us who view the sale of a well-loved yacht after 12 years as an event comparable with divorce, the whole business becomes rather unsettling.

The fact that the buyer turned out not to be a buyer at all but merely someone who was rather too enthusiastic, only added to the sense of desperation – particularly when I drove a long way to collect a cheque for the deposit and he explained that he didn't actually have the money – not as such, not at the moment and, well, he wasn't entirely sure when he would have the money.

But by this stage I had begun to realise that everything to do with selling boats takes place in a parallel universe – one where time is cyclical and nothing ever reaches a conclusion.

It is also a universe peopled by some real collector's items. Take, for instance the man who wanted a boat to die on.

Yes, I thought it was odd. But he was perfectly serious. He was very ill, he explained, and would never be cured because he would never again let a doctor near him. This was not unreasonable considering his experiences in the surgery: his last doctor had told him that unless he gave up sailing, he would be dead within a year. He did give up sailing, and promptly became so miserable that his wife left him. This, of course, made him even more depressed. By the time he came to see *Largo* he was in a state of terminal decline and clearly relishing every moment.

'She'll make a good coffin,' he said, wandering around shaking the rigging. When we set off for a trial sail, the feel of a tiller under his hand transformed his expression to one of supreme contentment – rather as if he was ready for the angels at that precise moment.

It was just as well that his offer was calculated on what he apparently considered to be his life expectancy. It meant I had no qualms about refusing him; apart from anything else, I was not planning to condemn *Largo* to a lingering death as well.

We took a trip down to the West Country with a 'For Sale' sign hanging in the rigging but found that it only turned us into a miniature Boat Show. People who walk around marinas the same way they walk around Seaworld came and knocked and looked and said, 'How far out can you go in it?'

We were happier with the market trader who raised the business of bargaining to the level of an art form. First, he arrived on the pontoon and blocked out the light: he was a very large man indeed. Then he stepped on the side deck and *Largo* – no lightweight herself – promptly heeled to 20 degrees. He took a look, he rattled the rigging. He offered to write a cheque.

What, no survey! Not even, 'I have a friend who knows about boats. Would it be alright if he came and had a look?'

No, 'I'll have to think about it and call you on Monday.' Instead, just a hand in the back pocket and a confident stare.

It was all a bit unnerving; I mean, what do you do? You have to take him seriously. We got to within £500 of each other which, on a £20,000 boat, is the price of pride.

He went and sat in his car and waited patiently. We sat in the cockpit and worried furiously. I went ashore and made an ostentatious phone call. He went on sitting in his car, watching. It was like playing chess with Kasparov, only bigger.

In the end *Largo* went to the couple who sat in the cabin and drank beer, looked at the pictures on the bulkhead, listened to the stories and grinned at each other in that way which comes to those who know they have simultaneously made an important discovery.

Tamsin said that out of all the dozens who had come and looked and poked and rattled over eight months, these were the ones, and as usual, in such matters, she was right.

So if you find yourself snug against the quay one day and a somewhat anxious young couple in a Rival 32 come ranging up alongside, please take their lines and give them a smile. *Largo* has a new life.

Beyond the Pale

Look, this is embarrassing. I've bought a catamaran. There, now it's out, and I feel rather as if I've admitted to eating peas with my knife.

Of course, it's all to do with conditioning: I grew up sailing a Folkboat out of Walton Backwaters. We even used to look down on Stellas because they had an extra plank and another three inches headroom. Caravans, we called them.

As for catamarans – well, they were completely beyond the pale. According to Father, catamarans either turned over or broke up. They looked like blocks of flats or giant insects and if they were not being sailed by crazed young men who kept being rescued saying, 'I'll get it right next time,' then it was by overanxious couples – she in pink slacks and he wearing a white-topped yachting cap with an anchor on the front.

And now, eight months after setting foot on a cruising cat for the first time, I have one of my own. She is a Heavenly Twins. She measures 8 m overall and just over four in the beam. She looks like a funny little duck sitting on the water and we are calling her *Lottie Warren* after my great-grandfather's ship – he would turn in his grave if he knew.

Just how this all came about so suddenly still has my head spinning. A week before looking for the first time into a catamaran cabin, and picking our jaws off the sole and our eyebrows off the deckhead, we had our hearts set on a 40 ft steel cutter (steel for safety and 40 ft to live aboard). When we found that the only one we could afford seemed to possess the sailing qualities of a galvanised bucket, we went to the Southampton Boat Show in a state of some despondency. And that was where we met our friendly devil's advocate. 'Why don't you look at a catamaran? They don't sink and there's bags of room.'

Over the winter we drove hundreds of miles looking at catamarans. We even drove to Lorient (the bootful of wine had nothing to do with it).

Worst of all, we devoured books on catamarans. Every one of them was written by an enthusiast gripped with the sort of fervour that would do justice to one of those religions which comes to the door with pamphlets on the Day of Judgement. In this case the irrefutable tracts began with, 'For thousands of years the multihull has been the vessel of choice for transporting people – and it still is.'

Then there was the photocopied magazine article by the man who went round the world singlehanded in a Heavenly Twins and, despite being hit by 'an absolute monster of a freak wave', he came through unscathed, the little boat surfing sideways with the breaking crest. The treacle fell off the table, though.

There was Pat Patterson saying bluntly that a catamaran is safer than a monohull; that of the 500 or so Heavenly Twins built so far, not one had ever capsized. This was brainwashing on a grand scale. Pretty soon I found myself doodling with comparative lists of advantages and drawbacks. Did being able to run before the trades at 10 knots without rolling the gunwales under, outweigh the lesser windward ability in heavy weather?

Was the problem of being wind-rode in a crowded anchorage really so great if there was also the option of sitting upright on the beach?

And then there was the test sail: 13 knots reaching into Chichester Harbour. The most I ever got out of *Largo* was 9.7 and that was with everything straining in a gale and lasted just long enough for the log to register the record before we went into the mother of all broaches.

But the little cat surfed on and on. I couldn't believe it. Nor, come to that, could the broker – although, of course, he made a reasonable stab at taking it in his stride.

All this helped a bit but there was still the problem of the pink slacks and the assumption that the real reason people buy catamarans is because they don't like all that 'keeling over' and the china horses falling off the windowsill.

So we went to the Owners Association Annual Dinner and Dance. This was another eye-opener. I had rather hoped that our fellow members would be impressed with our ambitious cruising plans. Not a bit of it – they all had plans of their own, which seemed to involve rather more mileage and

certainly a lot more sunshine. And when the main prize was awarded to a couple who had circumnavigated the globe, and accepted on their behalf by a couple who had just returned from three years in the Med, I became rather subdued.

Every time we changed places (the men moved two to the left after each course) people asked all over again, 'And when were you converted?' It seems that multihull sailors spend so much of their time justifying their boats to sceptical – not to say derisive – monohull owners that they develop something of a siege mentality. Not that I have, of course. *Dogwatch* is nothing if not a balanced view of the yachting scene.

But if you see a funny looking little cat doing 13 knots up the river, please be good enough to get out of the way.

Old Friends

It was called the Treasure Chest. It sat on top of the stall at the boat jumble with a price tag of £20, and it broke my heart.

To the people who passed by and peered, it must have seemed like some sort of a joke: just a plastic tool box – the kind with a handle on the lid and two trays swinging out to reveal the vaults beneath – and all of it entirely full of a greater variety of nuts and bolts and screws and clips and what-have-you than anyone might reasonably imagine.

But it was my treasure and, like the iron-bound chest of an elderly pirate, it had been with me for longer than I cared to remember. I knew every corner of its cavernous interior: the precise division of 'small screws' and 'large screws' and exactly what the function was of the one which was bent at right angles and flattened at one end.

I knew how the split pins escaped from their tray and where they went to hide. Unerringly I knew how the studding could be inserted into the old outboard bracket spring so the lid would close, and with my eyes shut I could find the secret place to press so that it would open again without spilling the whole lot all over the cockpit.

But it all had to go. That is the sort of sacrifice you make when you move from heavy displacement monohull to small catamaran: everything gets judged by its weight. Things like the chopsticks at the bottom of the cutlery drawer were allowed to stay because they weigh nothing at all and nobody wants to buy them second-hand at a car boot sale. Yet the fact that they're completely useless outside the Far East gets forgotten.

On the other hand, the very real prospect of one day finding a use for some small part of the lifetime of hardware in the Treasure Chest did not stand up against the argument that it weighed more than the kedge and there was nowhere to put it.

Besides, it was only the reserve box anyway – a repository for all things rusty and anonymous. If I wanted shining stainless steel with the nuts and washers already complete, I had the smart new one with a lid that opened like the back door of a Rolls. In fact months could go by without my dragging the treasure chest out from the bowels of the port saloon berth – it was just that I liked to know it was there. I suppose that it was a comfort in times of stress – as when hanging over the stern to assemble the self-steering, if something went plop, there was sure to be something else in the treasure chest to rescue the situation.

I tried to explain all this to the prospective buyers on the other side of the stall. I seem to remember saying, 'Just think how much that lot would cost you in a chandlery – that's if you could find it in a chandlery.'

Most of them agreed that this was unlikely. A few of them smiled sympathetically, as they would at visiting time. But eventually a grey-haired gentleman in a fading Breton cap nodded with deep understanding and gave me fifteen quid.

The wrench at handing over the Treasure Chest stayed with me much longer than the £15. But gradually, like a child growing out of his security blanket, I learned to live without it.

After all, *Lottie Warren* is as near to being a new boat as I am ever likely to get, and new boats do not tend to lose bits quite as readily as the home-completed jobs I had sailed before. And when something does go wrong on a new boat, it does not do to botch things back together with a collection of rusty oddments which started out doing something completely different. I mean you don't find those Boat Show salesmen holding their exhaust systems together with bits of the head, do you?

And nor would I consider holding *Lottie Warren*'s rectifier onto the engine with anything less than the approved Yamaha nut, until, that is, it leapt out of my grasp and disappeared down into the bottom of the casing.

Now this was by no means a new phenomenon. Indeed, much of the reason for *Largo*'s particularly heavy displacement must have been the number of engine bits that had found their way into the bilges over the years. One look into the oily murk invariably had me reaching for the Treasure Chest.

But this time there was nothing for it but to retrieve the original. According to all the laws of nature it should have been impossible; wedged sideways into a crevice, it could not be hooked out or prodded out. It would have to be lifted out.

And in the end that is what happened. It was lifted out with all the delicacy of a single grain of rice – thanks to those blasted chopsticks which had been uselessly cluttering up the galley all this time. Which means there must be a moral somewhere.

To Cap It All...

To the Fellows of the Royal Society:

Dear Sirs,
I am sure you will be delighted to hear that the borders of scientific knowledge have today taken a giant leap back-wards with the completion of the next stage of my work on the subject of lost hats.

You will recall my earlier work, which resulted in the publication of *Passmore's First Law of Lost Hats*. In this we examined the complexities of cause and effect which come into play whenever the wind pipes up and someone on a boat puts on a hat.

The breakthrough – which received considerable publicity at the time – came halfway through the first leg of the 1987 Azores and Back Race when the freebie sun visor donated by the race's sponsor ended up in the water some 300 miles west of Vigo, necessitating the vessel being turned around to retrieve it (three attempts) and providing a rather good excuse for coming last.

My own misfortune notwithstanding, that day will long be remembered in scientific circles for proving that, in accordance with the Laws of Perplexity, the velocity with which I reached for the hat was matched instantly by an equal or greater increase in the wind speed – the ratio, of course, being depen-dent upon the square of the surface area of the visor's peak.

Had the weather been less clement and had I been wear-ing a bobble hat, we now know that the increase in the wind strength could have been calculated just as exactly from the circumference of the pom-pom.

Other formulae relating to a range of headwear, from the chandler's nylon Breton variety to the heavy-duty woollen affair with earflaps and storm gussets as knitted by the more traditionalist Lifeboat coxswain's mother, are covered in Appendix XVIII. But the statistical analysis shows that in 99.8743% of cases, every type of hat is eventually lost over the side.

Further work, I happen to know, is under way to discover whether the new fleecy-type hats also comply with Passmore's First Law. However I consider such work beneath me since it is obvious that hats in shocking pink or luminous green fall outside the Laws of Good Taste and therefore need not concern us.

This brings me to the establishment of *Passmore's Second Law of Lost Hats*. This work deals with the relationship between the hat and the main or genoa sheet. It is, of necessity, a wider-ranging study by virtue of the fact that in aft-cockpit yachts it is the mainsheet which flips the hat over the rail, while in centre-cockpit designs, the genoa sheet emerges at the top of the table of probability (Appendix XXVI Sheets, guys, halyards & washing lines).

I was prompted to this avenue of inquiry after acquiring a centre-cockpit vessel after many years with the other type. In the past it had seemed that only spectacles exhibited any form of magnetism for the mainsheet. But, as will be appreciated from an understanding of the Principles of Exasperation, only expensive prescription spectacles vanish in this way. Cheap plastic sunglasses, particularly the type bought in seaside postcard shops after leaving the Ray-Bans aboard, go on forever.

Hats, however, are another matter and the study shows that every type exhibits an equal propensity for being caught between tacks and catapulted some considerable distance into the water.

Indeed my very first outing in my present yacht resulted in the loss of a much-treasured Lacoste woolly hat, which I like to think made me look like the most fashionable kind of New York mugger. It disappeared into Chichester Harbour during the first experiments with my new endless line headsail reefing gear.

Indeed, it was this endless line, being as short as only an endless line can be, which was the cause of much of the trouble – I mean the research. The Theory of Vexation tells us that circumstances such as a rising wind, when the wearer has to lean out of the cockpit to haul on the furling line, puts the hat directly into the path of the thrashing genoa sheet.

Classifying such instances over the past year put paid to one Marks and Spencer's linen peaked cap, two Milletts' woolly hats, three of Mr Musto's rather grand double thickness thermal affairs, and an indeterminate number of ridiculous sun hats which were asking for it anyway.

It is interesting to note that replacing the endless line with a longer endless line (which is, of course, an impossibility of terms) did not alter the findings. Indeed, it is now possible to stand in the exact centre of *Lottie Warren*'s cockpit, hauling on the line, and watch the genoa sheet make a determined lunge inboard to snatch one's hat into the water.

I have attached some preliminary work on this phenomenon (genoa sheets: alien intelligence or inanimate abuse?)

I await the comments of fellow Fellows with interest.

Yours, etc.

Tackling Everest

The dog stood on the deck and looked up at the quay. This being Rye at low tide, it meant pointing his nose high in the air – something which tends to make him look pathetically appealing at the best of times. To this he added an expression of intense concern as he measured the vertical distance between himself and the start of his walk.

We had known that one day it would come to this. We had taught him to climb on and off pontoons, in and out of dinghies, up and down companionways but never before had he come up against 12 ft of ladder.

For a time I had entertained the vague hope that he would prove to be one of those remarkable dogs who learn to climb ladders. I made a big production out of telling him about the labrador I once knew who could do it. But Blue just looked at me as if I was mad and continued to stare at the edge of Strand Quay – or as it had now evidently become, his personal Everest.

Of course there were alternatives: we could put him in his lifejacket and hoist him up by the handle on the back, but this would inevitably have disastrous consequences since one of the straps passed directly across his bladder and the walk was becoming more overdue by the minute.

We could put him in a rucksack: the idea possessed a certain charm and would make for some wonderful photographs, but the only time we tried this it turned out to be like stuffing an octopus into a carrier bag.

So we were left face to face with the inevitable: Blue would have to be carried up the ladder. Considering his size and his bad breath, he does not get picked up very often so he leapt into my arms with a good deal of enthusiasm.

It lasted just long enough to begin the crossing from the boat to the ladder – along 3 ft of single rope footbridge swaying like the ones in all those Indiana Jones films (I had just made the discovery that when drying out in a catamaran, you keep the warps taut or end up yards from the quay).

Actually I don't think it was the possibility of falling into the mud which upset him. Indeed, in the early stages, in between lunching off my ear, I suspect he was confiding, 'Hey, I can walk through this stuff, no trouble.'

But when we got halfway up and looked down, he suddenly lost his nerve.

In hindsight, it would have been better if the moment had not coincided with the discovery that my free hand was now gripping a rung somewhere down by my knees and, if we were going to make any more progress, it would have to be moved – something which was not going to be too easy since the other hand was full of a dog who had now decided he wanted to learn to climb ladders after all and appeared to have grown half a dozen extra legs for the purpose.

Tamsin looked down from above and said, 'Are you all right?'

Now, I never like to say 'No,' to questions like that. When I admit defeat, I like to qualify things a bit. However there really was very little to bolster the confidence. In the end I said, 'Er, I don't think this is going to work.'

It ought to have worked. Had I not carried enough shopping up and down ladders over the years? I was something of an expert in the art of climbing ladders one-handed.

All the same, I had to admit I had not carried my Tesco bags clasped to my chest with two feet of French bread resting on my shoulder and a damp nose of liver sausage nuzzling my ear. For one thing the centre of gravity would be all wrong.

There was only one thing for it: very gingerly I extended a finger from somewhere underneath the dog and felt for the ladder. Very softly I began the hypnotic chant, 'Good dog, there's a good dog, what a good dog...'

The wriggling stopped. So did the breathing. And the next few seconds did not, after all, find us falling headlong into the mud in a tangle of fur and recriminations. In fact we skipped up the last few rungs with a flourish, and Blue trotted off across the grass as if there had been no more to it than sniffing at the back door until someone let him out.

It had all turned out to be so unexpectedly easy that I almost looked forward to the return journey, when a happily exhausted hound would nestle once again in my arms and the audience of passers-by would be impressed all over again.

I was almost right. The only difference was that after the walk the armful consisted of one part dog to five parts mud. By the time we reached the deck, I might just as well have fallen in head first.

Pan-pan Medico

It is one of the laws of nature that toothache, like childbirth, much prefers the small hours. You can be brave about it – or at least you can be lazy, turn over and hope it will go away. But eventually there is only one recourse. I stumbled out of bed in search of aspirin.

The medical kit lives in the locker under the sink. It consists of a pair of two-litre ice cream tubs, one inscribed with the word 'pills' and the other called 'dressings'. Blinking under the glare of the fluorescent light, I ripped the top off 'pills' and started to rummage.

There were pills in there for seasickness, pills for inflammation of the muscles, little bottles of capsules for constipation and indigestion. There were ointments and potions and powders and something called Dr Collis Brown's Pills, which are apparently very effective for digestive disorders and sounded as though they ought to have come out of a patent medicine catalogue circa 1905.

But aspirin? No. Not even paracetamol. Just a battered bit of plastic and tinfoil with the word 'Hedex' perforated by a series of oblong holes showing very clearly that these were now Ex-Hedex.

This was something of a shock. I had always taken a certain pride in the medical kit, having carefully assembled it for the 1988 Singlehanded Transatlantic Race. With help from the RYA's *First Aid for Yachtsmen*, the *Yachtsman's Emergency Handbook* and a gung-ho Australian, who is a would-be yachtsman and conveniently also my dentist, I had set about collecting the wherewithal to perform any medical procedure short of removing my own appendix with a kitchen knife and a shaving mirror.

The dentist came into the picture after I first approached the doctor. 'Could you prescribe something to keep me going if I break a wrist, doctor?' I asked reasonably enough.

The theory was that a spinning winch handle seemed about the most serious catastrophe that I might hope to be able to cope with – icebergs and Newfoundland trawlers, I reasoned, were beyond the scope of even the most well-stocked plastic ice cream tub.

The doctor eyed me over the free calendar from the drug company on the edge of his desk, 'I will not have you taking prescription drugs without proper medical supervision,' he said.

– But what if I break a wrist or something?

'Then you take your aspirin and remind yourself you're British.'

Oh great, a doctor from the Captain Oates school of self-preservation. I went to the dentist.

What he gave me was still in the ice cream tub and un-opened six years later when the toothache struck. It had a long name which I could not begin to pronounce and it came in huge lozenge-shaped tablets which looked as though they might have been prescribed by a French doctor for the other end – or else, it occurred to me, an Australian dentist with a sense of humour. Anyway I took one and knew nothing until I woke up, recovered but dazed, the following morning.

All of which persuaded Tamsin to tackle the ice cream tubs. As the ship's medical officer and a qualified nurse to boot, she set about the job with a certain alacrity – even incredulity.

There were wound dressings in there which were growing their own penicillin. The scissors were rusted into a brown lump. The cotton wool looked in a worse shape than the oily rags I keep for the engine.

But then, as I explained, I hadn't needed the medical kit very much. Even all the way across the Atlantic there had only been one real emergency – when I overbalanced while taking a sun sight and, anxious not to damage the sextant, arrested my fall by wrapping my teeth around the headsail sheet, narrowly missing the winch.

There was a certain amount of blood but nothing you could actually bandage. In fact I was explaining this on the evening radio schedule when a fellow competitor, an American in a 30 ft Carter some 50 miles astern, announced, 'No problem; I'm a maxillo-facial surgeon and I've got a full operating kit aboard. If you heave to, I can be with you in eight hours – we'll lash the boats together and I'll wire up your jaw.'

I was grateful for the offer – especially as he said he didn't usually make house calls. But considering I had carried a spinnaker all night when he had been down to just a headsail, I was damned if I was heaving to. Besides, I felt I could soldier on just as long as I stayed off the oatmeal biscuits that Pete Goss had gone round the fleet donating out of his Royal Marine rations like some sort of handicap.

In fact, in all the years and the thousands of miles since, virtually all I have needed from the medical kit has been an endless supply of waterproof plasters. This I suppose proves that old law of nature; the one which states that in all things – from spare clevis pins to wire cutters – if you have them, you'll never need them. But run out just once...

Change of Life

'But what are you going to do all the time?'

It was not a question that had troubled us greatly.

Boredom had never been a problem on the boat. The problem had always been piling back onto the motorway on Sunday evening, particularly when a weekend of gales and rain had miraculously transformed itself into one of those breathtaking sunsets that appear on the Boat Show brochures.

So we have made the decision. We are not going to go home any more, and announcing it has produced a barrage of questions.

First of all we have to explain that we are going to move onto the boat permanently. We are going to embrace the live-aboard lifestyle. And why not? Other people do it – there are enough books on how to do it. In fact to read Bill and Laurel Cooper, you would think there was some sort of rush on, and that if we didn't book our patch of blue water off the palm-fringed beach someone in a Hallberg Rassy would get there first.

So we made our decision. We decided that what had been a detailed, but distant plan was going into action at once, before next summer.

And all our yachtie friends have been thrilled; 'You won't regret it,' they told us. 'If only we had done it sooner,' they said. But we found that explaining the logic to everyone else has been a different matter entirely.

For instance, how do you explain to someone who has just wrestled their mortgage down to manageable propor-tions, and is already casting around for a country cottage, that you are currently selling all your books at car boot sales and advertising your clothes in the paper.

'What, all of them?' At this point people turn to Tamsin for reassurance, 'Surely not your lovely red silk suit?'

Very carefully Tamsin explains the pointlessness of a red silk suit on a boat, even though it breaks her heart to see it on the 'For Sale' rail with a £25 sticker on the lapel.

Gradually the word gets around: John and Tamsin are going to live on a boat.

'Oh really, where?'

Well we're not actually going to be anywhere in particular. We're going to be sort of cruising around.

So somebody comes up to me in the corridor, prods me in the chest and says, 'Ah, so you're the chap who's going off to sail round the world?'

Well, not actually round the world – not as such, not to start with. At first we'll just be going round Britain.

There is a pause. The questioner digests the reasons why anyone should choose Britain instead of The World. Apparently it is the equivalent of Cunard announcing that the next cruise of the *QEII* will be calling at Clacton-on-Sea, Barry Island and Morecambe Sands.

Then they ask how long it will take.

About two years.

'Two years! But you can sail round Britain in a month, can't you?'

Well yes, technically you can, but... oh, never mind.

How do you explain to someone the delights of going slowly – of waking up on a weekday morning in a deserted creek and having breakfast in the cockpit while the water runs away, and goes on running away as if someone some-

29

where has pulled out an enormous plug, and eventually there is just the occasional rivulet where the curlews strut and pick... and the only sound is that peculiar sort of crackling that comes from drying mud? And what sort of explanation can there be for expecting to spend an entire summer making our way through the French canals – so that we will be lucky to reach Spain by the winter?

The next question is inevitable, 'Then how long are you going to be away exactly?'

Well, sort of indefinitely, really. We haven't thought about it. We're just going, that's all.

'Just going?'

Yes.

This is when they give us the odd look – the look reserved for the intellectually challenged. It is clear that people do not 'just go' – at least, not people who are this much past their gap year. There is the inference in that look of irresponsibility, of foolishness and everything else up to impending doom.

And yes, it is possible that it might all go wrong. Maybe we will get bored. Maybe we won't be able to earn a living. Maybe the confines of a small boat will indeed pressure cook the relationship until one of us gives way to that irresistible temptation to throw the other over the side.

But then again, things can go just as wrong without ever leaving home.

So in the end we are left with Tamsin's sister Judith and her question, 'But what will you do all the time?'

She has heard the tales of previous cruises. She has seen the photographs taken in the Brittany sunshine and she can guess a good deal. So she says, 'I suppose you'll just have nice breakfasts and drink wine.'

Well, not all the time...

The Pint Pot

To the designer it is the cockpit, a place of cunning helmsmanship, conscientious watchkeeping, furious winching and, sometimes, lunch.

To us it is the cupboard under the stairs.

You can tell the difference as soon as you lift the flap of the canopy: instead of the neatly coiled sheets, winch handles in their pockets, serious-looking arrays of instruments, all you can see are cardboard boxes. We have just become liveaboards and our belongings are living in the cockpit.

We knew this was not supposed to happen. We had read all the books and knew everything there was to know about a measured countdown to the final pushing off. We cannot even blame the unexpected opportunity to go three months ahead of schedule. The fact is that we just brought too much with us.

To be perfectly honest we do not need 100 books, and I'm not talking about Macmillan's and the Sight Reduction Tables but John Mortimer, Paul Theroux, William Boyd and Iris Murdoch. And who needs all that underwear?

We have enough underwear between us to stock a busy Knightsbridge boutique. They never tell you this in *Sell Up and Sail* but once you have sold all your winter coats and ball gowns, you are left with your underwear. No-one wants your underwear – at least no-one wants mine. Also there is the argument that, since you will one day require more, it would be foolish to throw any away. Instead you stick it in a plastic bag and say 'Don't worry, we'll find somewhere to put it.'

Result, a cockpit full of underwear.

And toiletries. We never realised it but both of us seem to suffer from a little-known psychological disorder which compels us to buy toiletries at every opportunity. With me it is toothbrushes and toothpaste – I am always convinced I'm about to run out and so every time I pass Boots some unseen force drags at my ankles and there I am with a bagful of plaque-attack and incomprehensible chemical formulae.

Tamsin has a similar problem with soap. She thinks she is buying it to give to friends. She is wrong. Meanwhile we may not be able to get at the bilge pump but we will go down smelling very sweetly.

The wine is something else. With considerable precision we had stocked the bilges, then laid in enough at home to see us through to the day we thought we were leaving, and then one of my last professional assignments took me to Calais. What was I to do? It is as easy to get out of Calais without a bootful of plonk as it is to come away from the Boat Show minus the plastic bag full of brochures.

And so, moving the case of slightly suspect Corbières which happens to have a very nice picture on the label, we reach the tools.

Well, I thought we were going to reach the tools. I took them home to mend the bicycle before advertising it in the free-ads paper. They must be around here somewhere...

But that, of course, is the trouble with the cupboard under the stairs. You start throwing things into it as soon as you move in and continue throwing things into it until the day you move out.

I once left a house with a removals van half-filled with stuff I swear I had never seen before, which duly disappeared into the cupboard under the stairs in the next house. All of which works perfectly well if you really do have stairs, and a cupboard underneath them.

If not, you have a problem. We realised this as soon as we planned to set sail and the mainsheet turned out to be underneath the box of computer manuals – which are far heavier than anything explaining the boat's systems.

Even that might have been manageable without the food. Seasoned yachties will nod knowingly over the problems of stowing the victuals. Anyone who ever embarked on an ocean passage with a full crew knows how difficult it is to find enough space for two beers per person per day for 40 days, and that is without worrying about the stick of bananas.

But try emptying all your kitchen cupboards, the fridge, the freezer and the fruit bowl and putting that lot into the galley lockers.

So where did it end up? Don't ask. Anyway, it's all being moved tomorrow. If it stays where it is nobody is ever going to take us seriously.

So we've already started to shift it. I have looked around the boat – from the bow locker which seems to be full of guitar to the one under the foot of the double berth which is packed with tapes we completely forgot we had ever recorded.

For the time being it's all going into the dog's cabin. I always said it was absurd that he should have one all to himself.

Just as long as we remember to lock away the tin opener...

What a Performance

It was the dog who realised it first, but then he is an animal and probably best attuned to the sensation of living in a zoo. For the rest of the crew, the truth dawned slowly as we left the South Coast with its marinas and deep-water anchorages and other devices for keeping a respectable distance between the yachtsman and the curious onlooker.

Once we entered the Bristol Channel we found ourselves up against a harbour wall every evening. And what is on the top of a harbour wall?

A curious onlooker.

We knew we need never be lonely again. There was always someone to talk to – at least there was always someone to talk to us.

Sometimes they had a genuine interest and a pertinent question, 'Excuse me, I hope you don't mind my asking but what is that white lozenge-shaped thing on the front of your mast?'

Alternatively they might just want to make conversation. 'All right for the dog... I said it's all right for the dog... your dog – likes it on the boat does he?'

And then there were the ones who pontificated, 'That's a catamarang (sic)... See the solar panels, they're for heating the water.'

And oh, how we longed for one of the many people who came to ask about the two propellers on poles at the back to return the following day loudly telling their families, 'Now the two propellers on poles at the back, they're wind generators. They generate the wind, see...'

It started at breakfast time and sometimes it went on until the pubs turned out in the evening. On occasions it seemed there must have been a queue up there – dozens of people patiently shuffling up to the edge to offer their pennyworth. And if, thrillingly, we appeared on deck, the commentators went into overdrive, 'What's he doing...? Look he's got a bucket... What's he want a bucket for ...? He's going to wash the boat... What, with a dirty old bucket like that?'

Periodically dialogue like this made me abandon whatever it was I was about to do and start roaming aimlessly around the deck, rather like a laboratory mouse who decides the progress of science can only benefit from the inclusion of a little random data.

And yet all this was rather sad because there had a been a time when we actually enjoyed being the centre of attention. In Weymouth one memorable Saturday morning, we entertained an entire row of fish and chip gourmets to an impromptu cabaret involving Tamsin giving me a haircut in the cockpit with the galley scissors. Alternatively we could get out our venerable hand-cranked washing machine, 'What's she doing? Looks like she's making butter...'

But all things are best in moderation and the constant chatter from somewhere above us eventually began to prove wearing. It was as if we had no peace and certainly no privacy.

The dog was the first to rebel. There he would be, lying in his figurehead position on the foredeck and someone above his head would say: 'Look there's a dog on the boat... He must be a sea dog... '

As long as the banter remained on this level, Blue was quite willing to maintain a haughty detachment, occasionally casting a disdainful glance aloft as if to indicate that he had heard it all before and it had not been particularly funny then.

However as soon as anyone tried to address him directly (Who's an old sea dog then?), he would instantly start barking, which did nothing for anybody's sense of humour.

Perhaps it was this that contributed to events reaching their lowest ebb the other day in Watchet. This former commercial drying harbour boasts a wall renowned for eating mooring lines, and it was while I was trying to rig every short length of chain and every bit of plastic tubing I possess, yet at the same time excuse myself to all those people who believe dockside bollards were intended as seats for crab fishing, that someone asked brightly, 'Where do you hail from?'

And then immediately afterwards, added, 'Sorry I asked.'

I had no idea I had become so obviously bad tempered and the realisation brought me up short. After all who wants to have people whispering about the harbour: 'Watch out for that daft old blighter on *Lottie Warren* – bite your head off as soon as look at you, he will...'

And besides there was also the one occasion on this coast when we were not up against the wall. In Padstow we found ourselves outside a beautifully restored gaff trawler – all polished brass and carved oak. She did not so much steal the limelight as block little *Lottie* from view entirely.

It meant that when I swung myself and the shopping onto the ladder and the predictable person stepped up to say, 'Excuse me, may I ask you about your boat...?' I detected an absurd flash of disappointment at having to say, 'I don't think it is *my* boat you want to know about.'

Ohm Sweet Ohm

We are thinking of renaming the boat *Sizewell B*. With two wind generators and 125 watts of solar panels, on a good day *Lottie Warren* could earn her keep supplying the National Grid – but that is what happens when you surrender yourself to Ohm's Law.

I once subscribed to the theory – well, more of a religion really – of the KISS principle: Keep It Simple, Stupid. This fundamental truth had been passed down through all the generations of sailing heroes but simplicity thrives best in the sunshine. Start fitting out a boat for the British winter, and decide to make her both a home and an office, and suddenly the fixtures start climbing the evolutionary scale faster than Dr Frankenstein's laboratory mice.

We want heat in every cabin including the head, which means it has to be forced warm air, which is going to need one amp. The computer takes another 1.4, the fridge at least 1.3, the tape player, the gas detector – all those lights... sometimes I wake up in the night and find myself doing mental arithmetic.

But that's progress for you. It began the first time I spent a night on a boat of my own. She was on the small side and very basic but she did have a 12 volt battery and two fluorescent strip lights in the cabin, and surprisingly cosy they made it, too – what with the spaghetti bolognese bubbling on the stove and the transistor radio playing *Friday Night is Music Night*.

I distinctly remember sitting there towards the end of the bottle of wine and thinking what a lovely boat she would be to live aboard. That was how naive I was then, or at least, how drunk.

Anyway, since I could not possibly destroy the moment by going to bed, I was still sitting there with a silly grin on my face when it dawned on me that the cabin no longer seemed quite so cheery, indeed it was beginning to look decidedly gloomy. In fact it was getting downright dark. The battery was dying.

There was, of course, nothing to be done about it but to go to bed. There was no way of charging the battery apart from taking it home and plugging it into the mains. That was the year the outboard acquired an alternator and I lost my innocence.

Since then, like virtually every other yachtsman, I have become a slave to electricity and the means of generating it. The trouble with this is that once there is a theoretically unlimited supply, I start to find all kinds of different ways of using it.

Yachting magazines do not help, nor do boat shows. It takes a purist of the utmost determination to turn his back on electronic autopilots and digital logs with maximum and average speeds, not to mention the joys of Muscadet that is colder than the bilges.

And so the boat fills up with wire. There is an interesting correlation between the yachtie with a new electronic toy and the child on Christmas morning: suddenly it becomes far more important to see the thing working than to read the instructions carefully and install the equipment correctly.

This means that the electrical system on a boat can become somewhat idiosyncratic, and once she has been through two or three owners, it graduates to the totally incomprehensible.

How often does the temporary installation 'just to try it out' or 'until I get around to buying a 5 amp fuse' still turn out to be in situ five years later? Besides, the whole electrical system was only temporary – dating as it did from the original owner who had bought a job lot of red wire which meant you could never tell positive from negative without a multimeter or blowing something up.

That was why I always felt so guilty showing prospective buyers around, I could cheerfully punch a button, point to the obediently illuminated display and never get around to mentioning that the whole thing only worked because I had tapped into the nearest point of the lighting circuit, and then only with the help of a reel of plastic adhesive tape.

When the surveyor came to look over her, his recommendations included, 'A qualified electrician should be engaged to tidy up the electrics.'

He was right of course – just as I am sure I am right to bring in an expert to turn *Lottie* from a basic weekend cruiser into a floating power station. Now I have regulators and dump resistors and current and capacity monitors and something called a buzz board, which sounds like high-level corporate gossip. The march of progress seems to have achieved a momentum all of its own.

I finally managed to stop it when the qualified expert had this idea that there will be such a huge electrical surplus we ought to install an immersion heater.

But I still have a recurring nightmare that one day I will wake up and hanker after paraffin lamps, a drip-fed diesel heater and an old Olivetti.

Life of a Seadog

The dog has his own cabin.

Yes, ridiculous isn't it? When we decided that Blue was to say goodbye forever to the Lone Valley Dog Ranch and become a regular member of the crew of *Lottie Warren*, we rather had in mind that he would remain as respectful and grateful as he had been during his occasional trips aboard our old Rival, *Largo*.

After all, during his tentative afternoon's introduction on the mooring, he had allowed himself to be swayed aboard wrapped in a towel like some sort of unaccompanied livestock for export.

When we took him out into the Solent for the first time, he soon added the command 'Lee-oh' to his 20 word vocabulary (along with walkies, lead, dog food, etc).

And when he spent his first night aboard, sleeping in a banana box under the saloon table lowered into its alternative function as double berth, he never so much as uttered a whimper – no matter what went on an inch above his head. In the morning we just slid him out again as you would the bottom drawer and he promptly came alive like something out of *The Nutcracker Suite*. But now that he has spent a good part of the summer afloat and acquired the confidence of a regular boat dog, he has begun to make his own arrangements.

We noticed the subtle shift when he discovered the benefits of marina living and stopped walking down the pontoons eyeing the water underneath and moving with the bow-legged gait of an arthritic tightrope walker. But it did mean that everyone looked and said, 'Look, there's a dog in a lifejacket.'

After a while we began to tire of this – the Crewsaver was not supposed to be a fashion item. We just thought that if ever he were to fall in, the prospect of seeing a small black head in the water could only be matched by the difficulty in pulling him out again.

Actually he has only fallen in once, and then it was only into the marina. But if you have never seen a dog trying to climb four feet of vertical glassfibre, you have not witnessed real panic.

But most of the time he treats life afloat rather as I imagine my grandfather must have treated his one week of the year chartering the old Xenia at Cowes in the 1920s. The sepia photographs show the old boy posing with his cronies by the wheel. They all wore identical reefer jackets, yachting caps and whites, and all appeared to be desperately trying to look as though they belonged.

Blue belongs. Every morning he takes his constitutional on the foredeck, does his bending and stretching exercises, and settles down to keep an eye on the world. From time to time people come past and say, 'Look, there's a dog in a lifejacket!' and he preens a bit and looks haughty, but mostly it's a matter of checking out the smells borne on the wind: mud, rotting vegetation, raw sewage – all the good things in life...

When the time comes to get under way he likes to stand up, hoist his tail in the wind and go down the river like a figurehead ('Oh, look, there's a figurehead in a lifejacket!') and it's much the same coming into port at the end of the day.

41

It is just unfortunate, that in between times, life afloat is interrupted by the open sea. The open sea is not something Blue cares for ever since a dollop of it joined him on the foredeck aboard *Largo*. At such times he likes to come back to the cockpit and sit wedged behind the helmsman's knees and look pathetic.

Still, it's all forgotten at the other end of the trip when the time comes to go ashore. Then he stands in the bow of the dinghy ready to leap for the jetty as soon as we get within ten yards – the fact that Blue can only leap two yards has yet to discourage him.

Coming back is more of a problem. This is because he is invariably covered in mud. We have tried to teach him to sit in the bow, but apparently his vocabulary reached capacity with the addition of 'Lee-oh' and he has to trample mud all over the rest of the dinghy first.

To begin with I thought this was a good way of cleaning his feet, until he finished off the job by doing a couple of circuits of *Lottie*'s decks as well. But, by this time, just as we began to wonder whether a dog on board was such a good idea after all, he saunters off to his cabin – his own 6 ft 6 in x 3 ft berth with his own red and yellow striped duvet (which he promptly kicks aside so he may dry himself more comfortably on the royal blue velour underneath). And there he stays until he hears the first stirrings from the next door cabin in the morning.

It makes you wonder what they mean by 'a dog's life'.

Whiff of Success

The essential statistic to remember is that there are seven million particles per litre of air over a land mass and only one million over the open sea.

This information I have on good authority from a Master Mariner and former officer of the Royal Fleet Auxiliary. He seemed mildly surprised that it should come as a revelation to the yachtsman. But the significance is positively cosmic. Armed with this one piece of knowledge, the navigator is instantly provided with a fail-safe back-up for GPS, Decca, RDF and any other complicated position-fixing system which might go on the blink when he least expects it.

For the wonderful thing about particles is that they activate not a set of recalcitrant microchips but the Mark One Olfactory Gland – in other words, the skipper's nose. What we have here – already installed and entirely free – is navigation by smell and we should not dismiss it.

The ancient Polynesian, voyaging far across the Pacific understood the particle principle when the trade wind brought the scent of palm trees wafting over the horizon. The Thames bargee relied on it, fogbound in the Black Deep: whenever the ship's dog started whining it was because he sniffed wet sand.

And it is no less valid today just because somebody has got around to counting all those particles. After all, every long-distance yachtsman knows that wonderful sensation, after weeks at sea, when all at once the breeze is filled with the perfume of vegetation and the imagination lights up with visions of green hills and wild flowers.

It's just that these days, with a liquid crystal display at the chart table solemnly counting off the miles to the waypoint, we tend to dismiss the evidence of the fifth sense. And what is more, we do so at our peril. GPS is nothing without the goodwill of the Pentagon, and Decca will beep its last in the year 2000. What's more, both of them are only as good as the electricity supply. Even a sextant is not totally reliable – at least not once it has been bashed against the side of the companionway on its first unaccustomed outing into the cockpit. And even if it does survive then Sod's Law dictates that the astronomical tables, stowed for so long under the quarterberth waiting for just this emergency, will emerge as a solid, mildewed lump. Yet there is very little that can go wrong with the skipper's nose.

I can't think why candidates for the Yachtmaster Offshore certificate are not already required to demonstrate the correct use of the nose in the same way that they are expected to navigate up Southampton Water without rising from the chart table. It need not be so very different: a blindfold, nostrils a-weather and the unmistakeable scent of Fawley oil refinery to port means 'steady as she goes'.

According to my friend the Master Mariner, certain equatorial countries can be identified by their smell at a range of more than 100 miles, and he recalled that once, when still the best part of a day away from Charleston, the lookout came in off the wing of the bridge and announced, 'I can smell America.'

'What does it smell like?' asked the officer-of-the-watch.

'Garbage.'

So, for the greater safety of future generations of seafarers, I propose to compile a new set of charts to be known as *Passmore's Particle Projection*. The essential difference will be that in these charts the land will be colour-coded. The eastern shore of Southampton Water, for instance, comes out as a dull grey – the colour of a Hamble mainsail cover after a season's production at the refinery.

Then, moving around the country we could have a rich golden brown for the scent of Cornish pasties drifting out to sea from Falmouth, the only town which seems to smell entirely of lunch from ten o'clock onwards.

We could have black for spilled crude oil at Milford Haven and the whole of the West of Scotland might reasonably appear in varying shades of pale gold, the hallmark of single malt whisky. Indeed it seems only natural that this tricky coast should benefit from such a precise navigational aid, enabling the connoisseur running up to the Sound of Islay to tick off the uncompromisingly smoky Laphroaig and the iodine and cocoa peatiness of Lagavulin before turning to port at the first hint of Jura's slight trace of ammonia.

Scotland's northeast coast, on the other hand, will be uniformly white – as in white fish.

Of course the best thing about Particle Projection is that it is user-definable. For instance, if you firmly believe that you can detect the smell of fish and chips anywhere within 20 miles of Scarborough lighthouse, then by all means get out the colouring box and set to work with the noble red of the Sarson's label.

It is infallible – a breakthrough which may yet go down in the annals of seafaring along with the discovery of longitude and the invention of Sikaflex.

At least, it will once they find a cure for the common cold.

Walking the Plank

You can tell a lot about a boat by her gangplank. In the Med, where they call it a passerelle, it can have a tasteful blue awning, a balustrade and wheels on one end. In which case the yacht attached to it is likely to have satellite communications, a Mercedes in a locker under the sun deck and somebody in a white coat holding a silver tray of champagne.

Our gangplank is not like that. Ours is more of a plank. It has a slot cut in one end to fit round the base of the pulpit, a bit of rope to hold it there, and one of the dog's discarded towels underneath to protect the gelcoat.

But I am as pleased about it as if it had come complete with a Royal Marines Band to play on the quayside each time I stride up it. Well, not so much stride up it as sidle – having waited to see if it will hold first the dog's weight and then Tamsin's. Actually it bends horribly and makes me think of the wording on the boatyard contract which says it is used at my own risk.

But none of that can take away the pride and sense of occasion I get from having a gangplank. I mean, would the Duke of Edinburgh have looked half as distinguished in his uniform of Admiral of the Fleet if he had had to get off *Britannia* by cocking his leg over the guardrails and stepping down onto a pontoon or – heaven forbid, picking his way across the decks of half a dozen destroyers before scaling a seaweed-covered ladder up the harbour wall to emerge finally on all fours at the feet of a family in Kiss Me Quick hats eating chips?

Certainly not; His Royal Highness had a gangplank – or in his case, a 'brow'.

But I am not sure whether he ever had the problems that go with it. For one thing there is the dog. A dog on a boat quickly comes to realise that his territory is bordered by the guardrails, in much the same way as his garden is bordered by the hedge. But take down one section of guardrail, give him ten feet of gangplank, and it is the equivalent of opening the garden gate.

To begin with Blue was content with the inboard end. He sat there rather in the manner of a security guard; it gave you the impression that he had a clipboard somewhere. But after a while he took to positioning himself in the exact centre, so that he then looked like a contestant in one of the sillier events in the local regatta.

This also was acceptable, even endearing. The trouble arose when he discovered that it was but a short step from the middle of the gangplank to the quayside, and no distance at all to the bench where people sat to eat their sandwiches.

It was after our third expedition to retrieve him that we began to think that maybe the gangplank was not such a good idea after all – at least not without some means of hoisting it up or swinging it inboard at will. Because the other thing to remember about a gangplank is that it represents power.

This was something which was demonstrated very forcibly to a friend who made the mistake of accepting a week's flotilla racing in Greece. Arriving in the typically picturesque harbour, the skipper moored alongside a large wooden ketch flying the Australian flag – the sort of boat that has acres of brass and varnish and ends up on all the

postcards. The flotilla crew duly stepped across onto the gleaming teak decks, filed down the passerelle – pausing to admire the Turk's heads on the handrail – and wandered off in search of lunch.

Returning sometime later full of dolmades and retsina, they were understandably miffed to discover that the Australian had withdrawn his passerelle and had apparently disappeared, which of course was impossible since he had to be on the boat somewhere.

After a good deal of hailing, he appeared in the companionway and announced that no, he would not be putting it out again for their benefit. He was fed up with people tramping all over his decks. To his way of thinking if people wanted to get ashore they should make their own arrangements. And yes, it was a matter of supreme indifference to him if people ended up being stranded through their own foolishness.

After such a good lunch, the flotilla crew felt the afternoon was turning into something of a disappointment: nobody would lend them a dinghy. The harbourmaster had gone home for his siesta. The fishermen were out fishing. It was not until the evening sun bathed the town with that golden light typical of the Greek islands, that the Australian also mellowed and allowed his neighbours back aboard – extracting abject apologies with every step.

He is probably still there, still peering through his brass portholes, looking for likely victims, and the awful thing is that I know exactly how he feels.

Life of Luxury?

As the owner of a luxury yacht, I would like to make one thing clear: the mildew in the back of the knicker locker is going to be dealt with just as soon as I get around to sewing a new bit of yellow cloth onto the end of the grossly frayed burgee.

For those readers who imagine luxury yachts do not suffer such indignities, I should add that *Lottie Warren* will only qualify as a luxury yacht if she sinks in some particularly spectacular fashion – possibly involving a good deal of NATO and certainly lots of helicopters.

Then the newspapers will recount in lurid detail that we have gone missing aboard our 'luxury yacht'.

You know the sort of thing, 'Two Britons were feared drowned today after their luxury yacht was reported missing in gale force winds and mountainous waves... etc...etc...'

Why is it that nobody ever goes missing in a modest family cruising boat?

Well, for one thing it is not nearly as interesting and anyway – apart from the occasional 'Captain Calamity' who sets off for Barbados in a converted trawler, navigating with the AA road map and getting pulled off every sandbank in the Thames Estuary – most yachtsmen do fall into a media niche. We do it for fun and we spend more on our hobby than people do on gardening or darts. Inevitably we have 'luxury yachts'.

There is absolutely no point in telling the man from *The Daily Gabble* that there is a steady leak in the deck join at the chainplates, the engine smells of hot diesel because you crossed the threads on the injectors, and it is best not to mention the problem with using the cooker on starboard tack because an apple has become inexplicably wedged down the back, nobody can reach it and you are still waiting for it to rot enough so you can flush it out with a hose.

If you try to explain all this you will merely make your mark in the cuttings library as an eccentric with a luxury yacht, 'Despite owning a luxury yacht, he attempted to play down his vast wealth...'

We know all about this since Tamsin, in a marina launderette in mid-winter, found herself being asked, 'Are you on holiday or are you just rich?'

She says she never really replied. She was sorting socks at the time, and you would have thought that that would be answer enough.

So what exactly should constitute a luxury yacht? If we can get this sorted out we can issue a set of guidelines to the newspapers and save a lot of embarrassment all round. My own view is that a luxury yacht has a crew. Indeed, it has a skipper in white ducks and someone with a silver tray and an ingratiating smile. Tamsin insists the inventory should include a dishwasher and an airing cupboard. I tell her she's not trying. She thinks again and comes up with a walk-in refrigerator and a spin-dryer.

Since we started on this we find we have a ready basis for dreaming up impossible luxuries without the inconvenience of compromising our philosophy that life should be kept reasonably simple. We can be disparaging about an ice-maker in the cockpit and salivate at the same time.

For instance, a luxury yacht should have the name picked out in gold leaf on a plaque on the side of the coachroof. She should have a full set of signal flags and someone to get up and scrub the teak decks early in the morning so that by breakfast time they have dried white and hard and gleam in the tropical sun.

The luxury yacht should have an ancient Scottish engineer named McTavish hidden away in the forepeak. He would wear slightly soiled white overalls and carry a small canvas toolbag and whenever I attempted to mend anything and inexplicably wrecked it beyond any hope of repair, McTavish would appear with his tap set and wooden-handled screwdrivers and say something like, 'Och Sorr, is the wee drive shaft oot o' alignment, then?' He would then set to, whistling soft Highland melodies and rescue the situation.

There would also be a boarding ladder that sticks out sideways so you can walk down it like stairs, and at the bottom, a varnished launch so large that you get into it by stepping on the gunwale.

And on board the luxury yacht nobody ever, ever says, 'I thought you made the dinghy fast. I couldn't do it because I

had the shopping/dog/water-can which is anyway still empty because we couldn't find the tap...' And even if they did, there would always be another dinghy in which to go and collect the first.

It would all be so different, and yes, it would all be so dull. Which is why, on board real luxury yachts everyone always looks so miserable.

And that is the end of the fantasy for today. If you will excuse me, I have to go and take the furling gear off the forestay for the third time in a week. Please don't ask why.

Breaking the Ice

The thermometer said -3.5°C. That was on the inside. Outside the ice rasped at the hull. We could hear it plainly through what suddenly seemed like a wafer of fibreglass.

We could not see what was going on outside because all the windows were solidly opaque from a night of frozen breath. Closing my eyes again, I tried to remember what on earth had persuaded us to winter in Spitzbergen. Except that this was not Spitzbergen. This was Swansea and we were supposed to be leaving in two hours.

I think the problem must have begun in childhood – this idea that there is something romantically heroic about winter sailing. I remember a family who lived down the road returning from a weekend on their 21 footer, and reporting that they had needed to sweep the snow from the decks before casting off. That was at Easter and I thought it the height of tenacity.

In a similar sort of fashion I have carried around with me for as long as I can remember various pieces of arcane advice for winter seafarers: always let a headsail flap before going about in order to shake the ice from it. Float a couple of planks at the stem to deflect ice floes drifting down on the tide. Avoid rolling hitches like the plague. All jolly useful stuff, you'll agree...

None of it, however, the slightest help on waking to discover the marina frozen solid.

Naturally the initial reaction was disbelief. Sea water does not freeze – at least not in South Wales. But this was not sea water. This was fresh water from the River Tawe; there was a barrier and two locks between us and the salt stuff.

I took the boathook and poked at it. Here was no fragile skin; this was an inch thick.

That part of my brain which thinks it belongs to Ernest Shackleton began making plans to get the stores off the ship and set up camp on the ice. I began to formulate instructions for the ship's carpenter on preparing the rubber dinghy for a voyage to South Georgia... And then we heard the noise: a

deep growling, crunching sound that chilled the spine – the
sea-angling boats were setting out, pushing and shoving out
of their berths, sending cracks racing across the surface and
leaving black trails in their wake.

Men with purple faces and gloves without fingers
laughed and fiddled with tackle. To them it all seemed to be
enormous fun, and certainly none of the boats appeared to
be holed or sank before they reached the lock.

Maybe we were letting the novelty get the better of us. We
started to prepare for sea; breaking the backs of the bowlines
in the mooring warps, yanking open frozen deck lockers –
persuading the engine to run for more than a minute at a
time. But when I put it in reverse absolutely nothing happened. It was all very well for fishing boats with 40 hp to
play at being icebreakers. *Lottie Warren*'s 9.9 hp outboard was
never intended for this sort of thing.

I revved at full throttle and somewhere under the ice the
water moved around. Above it nothing stirred.

Tamsin began to ply the boathook like a harpoon, jabbing
small, neat holes in the ice behind us. We balanced the idea
of waiting for the thaw against shunting backwards and

forwards with something akin to road rage until we simply smashed our way out.

Impatience won, as usual. It took about half a dozen attempts, and a great deal of wincing, but after five minutes we were one boat length out of our berth and still appeared to be watertight. All we had to do now was turn. Neither of us had the slightest idea how to accomplish this. At ice-breaker school they probably reduce the problem to one of pure physics: forces acting upon the vessel and whatnot.

I just recalled the principle that if you give a man a lever and a place to stand, he can move the earth. I stood on the foredeck and grasped the pushpit of the next door boat and set about moving Swansea Marina.

Well, that is how it began. *Lottie Warren* has a waterline length of 21 ft 6 in and that is exactly how much ice she began to shift. The din was rather like an elephant skate-boarding down a gravel drive. Great sheets of ice piled on top of each other and subsided, fissures fanned out and dis-appeared between the moored boats behind. By the time we ground our way to the lock, adding our own trail to those which converged from all directions to a form a dark pool full of floating shards like an over-enthusiastic cocktail, we felt as if we had achieved something rather heroic.

It would have been gratifying, for instance, to tell some-one about it – someone who only had a story about snow on the decks...

But the man in the fishing boat ahead of us just winked out of the hole in his balaclava and said, 'Bit nippy this morning.'

Rock-a-bye Baby

For some time now we have been loading the boat with books with titles like *Babies Aboard and Children Afloat*. For alternative opinion, we have *Family Sailing* and Dr David Lewis's rather more muscular *Children of Three Oceans*, as well as the sections on children in all the more usual guides to selling up and sailing.

We are, one way and another, not short of advice, and now we have a baby of our own so we can find out if any of it works.

Little Owen arrived in March in North Wales – somewhat unexpectedly as it turned out: he wasn't due until April.

And if anyone thinks I have been keeping him under wraps all this time, there is a very good reason, and not just an aversion to being given any more bootees with anchors on them: we wanted to take Owen sailing before passing any sort of judgement on the experts' views.

It would have been too easy to slap a 'Baby On Board' sticker on the cockpit coaming, hang a row of tiny vests from the guardrails and announce that we had an enthusiastic new crew member. After all, one thing all the books seem to agree about is that new babies are the ideal sailing companions: they require only to be warm, dry and fed; they stay where you put them and the rocking motion sends them to sleep.

To read some sailing writers, there is really nothing to it beyond a little common sense and the ability to pick Lego out of the cockpit drains.

But then I mentioned our new crew member to the readers of *The Daily Telegraph*. The reaction was instantaneous and startling: it was all hopeless, and more to the point, it was irresponsible.

A mother who had tried cruising with a baby and been forced to move ashore wrote us two pages filled with tales of colicky infants rousing entire anchorages at four in the morning, three-year-olds still unable to walk because they never got the chance to practise and the horror story of a couple marooned in their own private hell of Tobago because they inadvertently gave birth to a little tyrant, cannot take him to sea without help and, similarly, cannot inflict him on a crew.

Then there was the columnist in *The Guardian* who likened us to Nick and Jill Schinas, the couple rescued with their two children after a series of knockdowns north of the Falklands. Apart from the obvious dangers, she asked, why was this child being denied the simple pleasures of family picnics and feeding the ducks in the park?

It seemed that just bringing Owen home from hospital to berth B12, Conwy Marina instead of The Laburnums, Acacia Avenue was a crime against society.

There were times when we considered keeping him a secret – a sort of literary stowaway who would only surface when he had learned to 'hand, reef and steer'.

Of course the answer, like most things to do with boats, is a compromise: so far he has turned out to be not nearly as easy nor as difficult as either side suggested. For instance, it does not seem to matter to Owen that he lives with a piece of plywood to stop him rolling off the settee berth and under the table, or that his baby-bouncer hangs from the boom instead of a doorway.

He is warm, fed and dry, although he never seems to stay anywhere for long because for some reason we always want whatever happens to be in the locker underneath him.

However I would like to get my hands on whoever dreamed up the suggestion that the rocking motion of small boats sends babies to sleep.

We gave him a trial run – a gentle sail down to the fair-way buoy and back: he stayed in his car seat lashed in the cockpit just long enough for us to say, 'Look, he likes it' and take his picture. Then he howled.

Never mind, his first job is learning to smile at harbour-masters. All the books agree there is nothing that wins you a space in an overcrowded harbour faster than a gurgling blond baby. Later we plan that he shall graduate to working on surly Mediterranean immigration officials. Given his success so far (marina staff doing our laundry, harbourmasters waiving all charges, etc) we feel that he does possess a certain natural aptitude for the work.

Of course some aspects of the cruising life do become more complicated: like not being able to trim the genny because there is a multicoloured windmill sticking out of the winch, or finding the anchor locker entirely full of rather suspect little plastic bags each one claiming to be 'odour-free'.

And it is perhaps best not to dwell on what the dog thinks about having to share his cabin with hanging netting stuffed with an astonishing number of small garments, and every one of them covered in anchors.

Hot Gossip

Largo had a brick. There are probably not many racing boats which run to a house brick tucked away in a cockpit locker, but a rather opinionated friend had delivered it with such ceremony that I found myself unable to throw the thing away.

That brick did two Atlantic crossings and an Azores and Back – not to mention cruising Brittany, Normandy and the West Country. It was a well-travelled brick considering it never once did what it was supposed to do. It was supposed to heat the boat. According to the rather opinionated friend, a house brick placed over a gas flame will radiate heat far more efficiently than the flame itself.

Indeed, unlike the flame, a house brick can be wrapped in a towel and placed under the saloon table. The crew may then sit and warm their feet on the brick, and it will still be warm enough later on to go in a sleeping bag. A house brick, in other words, was as indispensable to a boat heading for the Grand Banks as a radar reflector or a fatalistic approach to life.

Actually I never got to use the brick. The North Atlantic that year was unusually warm so I cannot tell you whether the brick-on-the-cooker-heater works any better than the terracotta-flowerpot-on-the-cooker heater, which I understand is a distant cousin with its own, equally ardent, following.

But then I am probably not the best judge, having very nearly done away with myself when experimenting with the cooker itself as a boat heater. The logic was infallible: cooking always made the boat nice and warm, therefore the obvious way to warm it up was to light the cooker.

The subtle difference is that when whipping up the spaghetti bolognese, you do not stretch out on the settee berth between adding the mince and mixing the Oxo for a couple of hours' kip.

It was only later, on waking with the mother of all headaches, that I remembered what the science master had said about the process of combustion and the way it consumes oxygen in large quantities and replaces it with various gases quite useless for supporting life.

After that I decided a heater was a luxury anyway. It was all very well if you already had a fridge and self-tailing winches and an anchor windlass, but not really necessary for the proper running of the ship. Besides, I rather liked going down to the boat before Easter and putting one sleeping bag inside another and sweeping the snow off the decks in the morning. It made me feel frightfully keen.

Now, however, the heater has assumed an importance previously achieved only by things like the rig and the engine. Those early spring weekends were all very well when I could get back into a the car on a Sunday night, turn the knob on the dashboard to the stop at the end of the red sector, and emerge 60 miles down the motorway with the temperature on the inside somewhere up around Florida in a heatwave.

All I can say now is that Monday morning bears a distinctly different aspect when, instead of waking up to the friendly ticking of radiators, the day's herald is a drip of condensation falling onto the end of your nose and the first thing you see when you open your eyes is your own breath.

So we now have a heater. It was very expensive, terrifyingly sophisticated and, in the three weeks it has taken to get it working properly, I have thought a good deal about cheaper and simpler alternatives – everything, that is, except the brick.

I recalled spending a school holiday aboard a converted sailing lifeboat in the Oslo Fjord, when the only thing keeping out the onset of a Scandinavian autumn was a cast iron solid fuel stove in the middle of the saloon. It was supposed to run on coke but seemed equally happy with driftwood or even the contents of the gash bucket. It was the sort of stove that should have been surrounded by red-bearded men in oiled sweaters smoking enormous pipes, and you needed a 50 ft Baltic fishing boat to cart it about.

Then there was a lovely little brass gadget reminiscent of those old shell casings which retired admirals like to keep as doorstops. This one had a chimney on top and you opened a sort of breech and loaded it with a charge of prepacked charcoal as if you were after the Bismarck. It worked splendidly and suffered from only one rather fundamental drawback: the charcoal came in brown paper packets which tended to get damp and acquire the consistency of a paper bag from a Chinese takeaway just before the sweet and sour hits the carpet. And have you ever seen two pounds of charcoal upended on a settee berth?

Just in time, of course, the thing from the Boat Show worked and proved that progress does have its advantages. If I sit just so, a jet of warm air goes straight up my trouser leg, and you don't get that with a house brick.

Shower Power

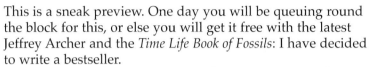

This is a sneak preview. One day you will be queuing round the block for this, or else you will get it free with the latest Jeffrey Archer and the *Time Life Book of Fossils*: I have decided to write a bestseller.

Now I know there are some yachting columnists who think they can make their fortune with a sailing Aga Saga (or, as it should be termed, All-Brass Taylor's Tale) but what the reading public really need is the *Good Shower Guide to the Ports and Harbours of Great Britain*.

The idea hit me the other day like an icy blast. Actually it was an icy blast. The 50 pence worth of hot water had run out after 42 seconds instead of three minutes, or possibly this was my own fault because I had spent two minutes 18 seconds working out how to adjust the temperature control.

Anyway you know the feeling: covered in fragrant hair-and-body shower gel, lovingly distilled from the essence of a hitherto undiscovered South American lichen, corrected for pH balance and developed without cruelty to anything – or, in other words, soap – I suddenly found myself faced with three choices.

I could stay under the sub-zero deluge and try to fight off the heart attack by sheer willpower. I could drip my way to my trousers, fill the pocket with soap while discovering that I did not, after all, have another 50p piece, and then debate further possibilities. I could dash for the steward wrapped in a towel, or put my clothes back on and wander stickily but with dignity into the bar? Or I could just stand there and rage at the injustice of the universe in general.

The point about all this is that I did not need to go ashore for a shower at all. We have a perfectly good shower on the boat.

Well, that is not entirely true and like many of the happiest accidents in history it is the reason why this definitive work is being undertaken: *Lottie Warren*'s shower is rather unusual.

We tried terribly hard but there was nowhere we could put a water heater where it would not either melt the head-lining, toast the back of the neck of anyone sitting at the saloon table or empty the water tank while heating up 50 ft of pipe.

So instead we opted for two thirds of a shower. There is the bit that pumps the water in and the bit that pumps it out, but for the heating element we rely on a boiling kettle to a gallon of cold in a jerry can and stick the inlet tube into that. It works rather well.

Oh, all right then, it'll just about do if there are no show-ers ashore. Which is where we came in. It is entirely possible that by the time Tamsin and I complete our circumnavigation of the country, we will have experienced the best and the worst that marinas, yacht clubs and the municipalities of the UK can offer.

For instance, there is the little unisex chalet on the quay-side at Rye where you may luxuriate in unlimited hot water. The council also thoughtfully provides not only potted plants and pictures on the wall but also a bolt on the door so that the next crew have to wait their turn.

Then there is the lady at Weymouth who runs the showers rather in the manner of a cloakroom attendant at an elegant but discreet West End hotel. She keeps a visitors' book and remembers boats from one year to the next. Last time we gave her a box of chocolates.

But it would be unfair, at this stage, to name the yacht club maintenance man who started out by explaining that the reason the showers were cold was because this was the first time they had been used this season, and then, when they fired superheated steam across the room, that it took time for the boiler to settle down. Or the little man I found round the back of another quayside premises with a screw-driver. He was already looking slightly startled after the shriek which accompanied the instantaneous transformation from Gas Board advert to Edwardian prep school.

'Did you do something to make the water go cold?' I demanded with what I thought was great charm and under-standing.

'I only...' he stammered, 'I mean I just turned this switch here...'

Oh, we'll see them all before we're done. The irritating little buttons you have to lean against or else the water stops every ten seconds, the trough in the middle of the floor where halfway through the proceedings the water suddenly gushes up, and your shoes float off like a pair of lighters with a severed tow. The exotic brands of shower gel left by passing crews from Estonia and Poland. The lost socks...

Readers wishing to reserve their copy should send a jam jar full of continental shower tokens which don't seem to fit anything, but which they can't bring themselves to throw away because one day they mean to drill holes in them all and make penny washers.

Whether the Weather...

Here, at the cutting edge of technology, we have a new device on test. Believe me, this is really exciting; even the technical editor hasn't got one of these. It is called The Canadian Weather Stick. It is a stick and it forecasts the weather – at least it does in Canada.

Not here though. Here it only forecasts rain. Maybe I failed to follow the instructions correctly: 'Hang your weather stick on an outside wall or door casing...'

I lashed it to the pulpit with PVC tape, and if it was not so obviously made of wood, people might mistake this new appendage for the 'active antenna' belonging to something electronic and expensive.

As it is, the weather stick points down for rain and further down for more rain and makes the boat look like an overgrown cottage garden – and we still have no idea when we shall see the sun.

But that is the wonder of weather forecasting: it is so inexact that even the most arcane device is bound to be right some of the time. Take, for instance, the gadget we found outside the marina office in Fleetwood: a stone hanging on a string. The accompanying instructions explained, 'Stone wet – rain. Stone horizontal – gales. Stone invisible – fog...' The whole thing was delightfully simple and surprisingly accurate; you could make your own.

On a slightly more technical level, one might consider pinning photographs to the bulkhead. I once saw this work terribly well with the skipper's three grown-up children: 'One son curling slightly – warm front approaching. Two sons curling – precipitation imminent. Two sons and daughter rolled up like an old chart – three reefs and fresh neck-towels please.'

The system is certainly as accurate as the little brass disc we had for Christmas the year before last. According to the instructions, you have to set the barometer reading on one scale, the wind direction on another and, depending on the pressure trend, read off predictions ranging from 'settled, fine' through 'changeable, some rain' to 'stormy, much rain'. Admittedly, by the time you reach this last one, you have a glass which has plummeted to 982 mb (and still falling) so it should not really take a novelty from Nauticalia to predict the end of the world.

But then, we also have one of those electronic barographs which flash up helpful pictures of the sun or an over-dram-atic rain cloud like the ones they have on television. These gadgets are a boon to people whose knowledge of weather lore is restricted to appreciating the comely forecaster's pro-file as she chatters on about 'blustery showers on exposed coasts'.

Of course it is entirely possible that the chaps at the Met Office have one as well, and I am certain there is one on the end of that premium-rate phone line – I used to call with such enthusiasm back in the days when somebody else paid the phone bill.

I stopped calling it when I realised I had stuffed £5 into a phone box to get bulletins for so many days ahead that the predictions left the realms of forecasting and might have qualified as hopeful prophesy.

And besides, I asked myself, what was wrong with the BBC? Well, not to put too fine a point on it, the problem with

the Radio 4 forecast is that it arrives all bright and cheery in its little bobble hat at 0555. The way we look at our cruising now is that if we have to be up at 0555, something has gone seriously wrong at the planning stage.

For a while we thought we had the answer with a little radio cassette recorder which had a built-in clock. I was so pleased with it, I made a special seven-minute tape specifically for recording shipping forecasts without flattening the batteries.

This was all very well except that two minutes after Malin Head (W 6 rain, falling quickly) the tape ended with a resounding click, which echoed through the boat as effectively as an alarm clock.

We tried putting the tape recorder in the locker under the sink, wrapping it in a towel in the sail bin, even burying it in a holdall with the spare pillows. But, no matter how muffled, that little click cut through the last wisps of sleep like a gale warning in the middle of *Woman's Hour*.

In the end there was only one answer: we would have to get a Navtex, and there it sits above the chart table, ready to hoover up shipping forecasts with silent and effortless efficiency.

Except that it doesn't – something to do with the way I installed the aerial, apparently... or at least, with the way I extended the cable with a bit of old co-ax which had been sitting in various bosun's lockers since 1979.

Of course, this being a centre-cockpit boat, I could get a shorter run if I took it to the pulpit instead of the pushpit – and, yes you've guessed it, I just so happen to have an active antenna up there all ready.

And I bet there's nothing like five volts to jolly up a Canadian Weather Stick.

Hose-anna

When I get to Heaven there will be a hose there. It will be just long enough but not so long as to be unruly. It will be attached to a tap. The tap will work.

Ah, but I can hardly wait...

My relationship with dockside hoses – never exactly harmonious – has fallen to a new low following a particularly ugly skirmish at Carradale.

It was one of those bitter, drawn-out encounters with both sides already exhausted by the years of conflict, but so poisoned in their minds that they will fight themselves to a standstill rather than admit defeat. In the end they can do no more than glare at one another, panting impotently, too spent to strike the final blow.

Except that on this occasion one of three jubilee clips slipped off and the water went all over my feet.

Those whose non-sailing and slightly anxious aunts give them weighty books on seamanship for Christmas know that fresh water figures prominently. There are dissertations on the correct way to store it, descriptions of half a dozen different methods of collecting it and even an explanation of how to make the stuff.

Very little, you observe, about what to do when the tap is a couple of feet down a dank and rusty hole and the only way to keep the hose attached to it is by lying on your face on the quay and keeping your hand there. And certainly nothing about maintaining a proper perspective on the universe when the clip you are not watching slips off and turns the filthy quayside into a wet, filthy quayside.

For most of us, the problem dates back to the age of about eight, when a lad first discovers that his parents are astonishingly pleased at his enthusiasm for the more exciting chores. You can see the downward spiral beginning any sunny weekend. The grown-ups sitting in the cockpit, glasses in hand, while a small lifejacketed figure trots off down the pontoon full of self-importance.

Ten minutes later the hose has jumped out of the filler, and swept once and with devastating effect across the cockpit before coming to rest aimed squarely at the open hatch over the skipper's bunk.

'It wasn't my fault,' comes the small voice from a safe distance. 'The hose jumped out.'

The fact that every hose is a living thing, possessed of a difficult temperament and a wicked sense of humour, is beyond doubt. What other explanation can there be for the way you can coil it neatly onto the hook below the tap, and then come back ten minutes later to find the wretched creature already engaged on chapter two of *Knots and Fancy Ropework*?

The fact that I admitted defeat years ago and bought one of those collapsible jobs on a reel counts for nothing. My hose clearly feels it owes me no allegiance whatever: I have yet to find any tap which it will condescend to fit without recourse to jubilee clips and skinned knuckles. Then, when the time comes for it to go back on its reel, it suddenly finds itself miraculously full of water and won't fit.

I suppose all these years of anxiety were really only a preparation for the day I would come face to face with the Godfather of all hoses. This revered being lives in some splendour in Liverpool's Albert Dock and I would not have believed such a magnificent monster existed.

The Great Hose of The Mersey is about the diameter of a trainee fire-hose and when the harbourmaster said there was a tap, he somehow forgot to mention that it was on a standpipe... in the road... not even in the dock at all.

In fact we needed three hoses – and three contractor's men to carry them – and then we had to have the key for the standpipe and an iron bar to show that this was serious engineering work being undertaken.

It took something like three quarters of an hour before the first drop of water made it to the tank. Foolishly, in the euphoria of the moment, I allowed myself to wave cheerily to the contractor's men and promise to leave the hose on the pontoon. It was a bit like promising the snake-keeper at the zoo that you'll put the king cobras back when you've finished with them.

Hose-anna

The whole business was all most unfortunate, what with tripping over the rampant coils and nearly falling in, and the people walking past wincing at some of the language and, of course, the wet feet...

In the end I walked off in a huff, squelching slightly and leaving the thing writhing away to itself and dribbling with unseemly satisfaction.

It is not, of course, the end. The Carradale Hose with its secret beginnings in the bowels of the quay, its leaks, its joints and its natural abhorrence of that enemy of all hoses 'Water Pressure', has proved to me that I am really engaged in some sort of mystical quest. One day when I have battled hard enough, and become wet enough, I shall attain the holy grail.

Or at least a watermaker.

Doggone

It has been suggested that the name of this page should be changed. We no longer have a dog to watch. Blue, who eventually grew to accept stardom as no more than his due, retired gracefully to the obscurity of the Scottish Highlands at the end of the summer. And we are left to make spluttering apologies to his fans.

'How's the dog?' people ask when we arrive somewhere new. Not, 'How are you?', you notice. Or, 'How's the boat?' Or even, might I suggest, 'How's the baby?'

But then the baby is part of the reason for the dog being put ashore – that and the practicalities of four of us on an 8 m boat, not to mention all that hair blocking the pumps and the way the companionway always seemed to be full of dog... and his nocturnal wandering.

In fact it was this last little failing that started us thinking about his future even before the baby arrived.

The problem was that Blue had his own cabin and was expected to give it up when guests came to stay. You would have thought that he would have been content. I mean, how many dogs get a 3 ft x 6 ft 6 in berth all to themselves?

But Blue preferred the saloon settee. He used to creep out there in the middle of the night – which was fine until Tamsin's pregnancy advanced to the stage where she began to make the customary visits to the head. Then Blue would bolt back to his cabin, leaving only a patch of suspiciously warm Dralon as evidence.

Such was the routine when my oldest son Olly came to stay. Olly duly took over Blue's cabin and Blue moved with his bed onto the saloon settee for the night.

It was some time in the small hours, when the brain (both human and canine) is at its lowest ebb, that Tamsin rose from her bed. In an instant the dog was awake, realised he was in forbidden territory and, with a single bound, was gone.

A second bound took him back to his own berth. On this occasion there was someone else in it; someone who was peacefully asleep with absolutely no idea that at any moment a large black dog would join him in something of a hurry. Sure enough Blue landed on the precise spot where his bed would normally have been. The precise spot was occupied by Olly's stomach.

The pandemonium which followed was magnificent – even Wagnerian. The memory has kept us entertained on dull winter evenings ever since. But Blue never saw the joke. This was a shame. Even Olly saw the joke eventually.

But would it be a joke when we had a baby in that bunk? And besides, what of the more distant future: was it really fair to take an elderly mongrel who had known only paltry British summers and expect him to acclimatise to the burning heat of the Mediterranean? And given Britain's archaic quarantine laws how could we ever come back?

We began to look for a new home for Blue. We put up notices in yacht clubs, 'Boat dog free to good home. Well used to dinghies and ladders. 24-hour bladder'.

Whenever an appreciative audience gathered at the dockside to applaud the dog who lay passively across my forearms as I climbed ten metres up a slimy ladder, my response suddenly became, 'Do you want him?'

Oddly, nobody did – not when they saw him make for the nearest lamppost and stand there on three legs for a quite astonishing length of time.

For there was no doubt that Blue had adapted to boat life better than we ever dared hope. Maybe he felt some obligation after we had gone to all the trouble of swapping a monohull for a catamaran just because we hated to see him skating across heeling decks, desperately trying to dig his claws into the fibreglass.

His vocabulary expanded to include a few basic nautical terms. We could tell him to board the dinghy and he would launch himself head first. When the resulting tidal wave settled, we could tell him, 'Blue, get in the bow', and he would comply, putting all four muddy feet on the thwart in the process.

He learned the hard way to wait until he was told to disembark (which was also how he learned to swim) and he learned that when anyone said, 'Oh look, there's a dog in lifejacket', he was expected to affect a look of disdain as if he had heard it all before, and what was so special about a dog in a lifejacket anyway?

But there must have been something because *Country Life* sent a photographer all the way to L'Ancresse Bay in Guernsey to take his picture. We have it still. It shows Blue staring boldly at the horizon with an expression not at all unlike Trevor Howard's when the clouds parted to show a moonlit Cape Horn to starboard.

That is how we like to remember Blue, although I suspect that now he is lying in front of a log fire trying to forget.

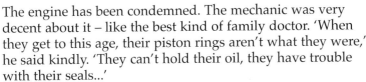

Farewell Old Friend

The engine has been condemned. The mechanic was very decent about it – like the best kind of family doctor. 'When they get to this age, their piston rings aren't what they were,' he said kindly. 'They can't hold their oil, they have trouble with their seals...'

What he was building up to saying was that the end had been a merciful release – that there comes a time when finally you have to let them go; it may be hard but it is for the best.

And I have no doubt that he is right. The little Yamaha 9.9 hp had suffered long enough. With its oil streaks and scuff marks and chips where once there had been gleaming white paint, who could blame it when one day the will to start simply evaporated.

So why is it that I have this urge to say 'no' – to insist that my faithful little Japanese friend deserves one last chance? Why this sudden compulsion to pay whatever it costs, demand a transplant, order spare parts?

The trouble is that like all the greatest partnerships, this one was forged in adversity. The very first time we met, down at Multihull World at the shallow end of Thornham Channel, it drove us off the mud. Well, actually it drove us onto the mud first, but that was my fault.

At full revs, forcing the water out behind us like a mill-race and with the whole boat vibrating to the tune of internal combustion, that little engine has driven us off the ground in more places than I can immediately recall.

Indeed, if you go and look at St Osyth Creek at low tide you will probably find the twin tracks of our keels still there, so deeply were they etched as we staggered the 50 yards or so back into the channel.

But that was only one side of the relationship. We had our differences too. There was, for instance, the business of the fussy carburettor: was it really necessary for it to reject entire consignments of fuel just because of the merest traces of sand, salt water, and filth? And where was the sense in deciding, as we negotiated the lock at IJmuiden, that it didn't like the setting for the idling speed?

I suppose at least that one gave me the valuable experience of commandeering another vessel. Indeed I startled myself as, with a briskness that would have stood me in good stead on an 18th century quarterdeck, I ordered the Swede we happened to be alongside to look sharp and tow us out.

It was after that particular episode that the engine and I had the first of our long talks. These tended to be one-sided affairs with me doing the swearing and the engine coughing a lot. I admit now that this was a mistake. Like an unhappy husband who can pinpoint the exact moment when the marriage began to go sour, I believe the trouble in Conwy had a lot to do with the trouble at IJmuiden.

There were two years between them but an engine never forgets and I know of no more vindictive way of making a point than staying in reverse when the gear lever says forward.

For instance I do not recall Noel Coward saying 'Full ahead both' down the voice-pipe only to have a disembodied whine come back to him saying, 'No, why should I? Do it yourself.'

By which time, in my case, we had reversed smartly into the boat behind, and I know it was deliberate because that one belonged to the sailing school and never ever did anything like this.

Since then things have not been easy between my engine and me. It has stopped inexplicably in places as diverse as Liverpool and Leeuwarden. It has failed to start in the North Sea shipping lanes and has given me an intriguing taste of what it must be like for a goldfish to swim up a fire-hose when it failed just as wind and tide combined against us in the Orwell.

And now I sit in front of a pile of brochures trying to choose a new one. Words like 'reliability' and 'performance' leap out of the pages at me. There are girls in wisps of Lycra and finely muscled, suntanned chaps without a trace of oil under their fingernails.

At the moment I am torn between Mariner, which features Scuba divers playing with dolphins on the cover, and

Honda's reflections in a peaceful fjord. But I suspect the real reason it is taking so long is that first I have to come to terms with this enormous burden of guilt.

Somehow it is not good enough to say that I am buying a new engine because the old one doesn't work any more. I should have looked after it better. I should have bought it more expensive oil – new filters instead of cleaning the old ones... I should have remembered its birthday...

But I don't suppose things will be any different with the new one. To begin with it will probably work – so I'll think of it as just another piece of machinery.

Love Thy Neighbour

The curse of the stones hung from the pulpit. It took me a while to realise that was what it was – a curse. But what else is one to make of finding a string tied to the pulpit and on the other end of it, lurking under water, a bucket of stones?

I have been waiting ever since to wake up in the middle of the night and find the bedclothes afloat. It saddens me to admit this but *Lottie Warren* had made an enemy. Actually this was more to do with my reaction to the crew on the other side of the harbour, with their raucous laughter and endless, doleful folk songs.

Anyway, not being much in the mood for somebody else's party, I staggered out of bed and deployed my patent cockpit party pooper: the 10,000 candlepower spotlight. It rarely fails.

There was a time, of course – back in the days when gentlemen went sailing in grey flannel trousers and you needed binoculars to read the name of the only other boat in the harbour – when yachtsmen were not greatly troubled by their neighbours. Now we have the same sort of problems that make judges shake their heads over human nature before binding over both parties to keep the peace.

We think we go sailing for the solitude, and yet we end up moored six deep with total strangers tramping across our foredecks and the next-door domestic crisis clearly audible through two skins of fibreglass – and that is without counting the party which goes on noisily into the small hours.

The folk singers were a typical case. They had a wide repertoire and an apparently endless fund of hilarious jokes, and it was a warm starry night so the party took place on deck.

Maybe it's because I'm a miserable old killjoy that I dislike other peoples parties but over the years I have had cause to investigate a range of alternatives to the traditional banging on the ceiling with a broom handle.

Certainly there is not much point in a polite request for some hush if you have to yell it across the harbour. I remem-

ber this getting completely out of hand once in Cowes.
Maybe it did serve me right for going there in the first place;
but sometime around midnight the crew of a 45-footer
returned from the pub and decided to continue the jollity in
their raised centre cockpit.

After the tenth burst of raucous laughter, there was a
shout from the forehatch of a little Westerly. 'I say, do you
mind – some people are trying to sleep.'

The skipper of a dignified Hillyard added his pennyworth
– something about 'a little consideration' and then a man in
an impossibly small motorsailer called out something about
'just because you've got a bigger boat' – which brought the
immediate rider from the companionway of an old gaffer
that 'it's probably
chartered anyway.'
By which time, of
course, the whole
marina was
awake and the
complainants
were making
rather more
noise than the
offenders.

I like to think I managed things rather better in Holland the other year. We were moored in a delightful spot just by the bridge at Goes when at 0300 the local nightclub turned out and half a dozen of the revellers thought there could be no better way to round off the fun than by jumping from the bridge into the canal – right next to the little English boat.

I was terribly polite. I smiled as I stuck my head out of the hatch – after all I was a guest in the country. With the utmost kindness I suggested that perhaps now might be a good time for everybody to go home to bed.

We awoke the next morning to find ourselves gently bumping into the adjacent boat; someone had untied a warp. If they had known how to dismantle a bowline, they would probably have cast off another one as well – and heaven knows where we might have started the day.

Which all goes to show that there really is very little you can do at the time. Complaining at the height of the festivities only seems to demonstrate what a great time everyone else is having and how you probably went to bed at 2200 with a cup of Bournvita.

No, this is a matter for revenge and it must wait a suitable interval. Apart from anything else, the Black & Decker job which seemed so attractive in the heat of the moment would probably look rather foolish when raised as evidence of criminal damage.

But a bucket of stones hanging from the pulpit – now there is true poetry. So utterly harmless, yet such sinister overtones...

And, rather in the way that an apprentice witch might be given a holiday project, one could even concoct variations on the theme: a neatly cut piece of turf on the stemhead, perhaps.

I shall give it some thought: already I have looked through the index in the Almanac (under spells, incantations, etc).

Deceptively Spacious

It was when we ran out of stowage space that we realised something was wrong. Was it unreasonable to possess 50 tins of food and 47 jars (from peanut butter to olive paste)? Were we somehow profligate in wanting to take with us 206 books (*Chambers Dictionary* to *Sell Up and Sail*)?

Worst of all, the problem arose not because we were moving onto a boat but off it, and trying to fit everything into a house...

No, we couldn't believe it either. But *Lottie Warren* is spending the winter ashore, and we have a new baby arriving any day so this seemed like a good time to rent a cottage with roses round the door and a huge wood-burning stove in the dining room and spread ourselves a bit.

And we have been considerably shaken by the experience. Nobody warns you about doing it this way. When you move from a house onto a boat there are books to tell you that it will be traumatic, that the loss of routine may destabilise the steadiest character – even that leaving behind the garden may lead to symptoms of bereavement.

But reversing the process should have been so simple. The cottage was only half a mile from the mud berth, a friend volunteered a van, and with our minimalist lifestyle – not to mention the constraints of living aboard an 8 m boat – this was one move which should not have qualified as second only to divorce in terms of stress.

I suppose the problem was that we had never actually moved aboard in the first place, at least not all at once. We just loaded more and more onto the boat for a couple of years – and then added what we could get into the car when we gave up work – and for three years since then we have been gradually topping it up and repainting the waterline.

Getting it all off in a morning filled the Transit van. It also filled the cottage. Clothes were the most astonishing: what had squashed down perfectly conveniently under a bunk suddenly filled a wardrobe and two large chests of drawers – not to mention a pair of sailing bags on the landing.

For a year and a half Owen had been content to have his clothes stuffed in nets around his bunk – for one thing it meant he could amuse himself in the mornings by pulling them all out. We never imagined that, neatly folded, they would fill a tallboy.

And then there was the appendix to Parkinson's Law: mess multiplies to fill the space available for it. Aboard *Lottie Warren* the remains of breakfast on the table could make the saloon look like a bomb site. Yet, after living in a house for a week, we were suddenly startled to find we could hardly move for clutter.

On the very first evening, Tamsin turned round, saucepan in hand, in a kitchen six times the size of *Lottie*'s galley and solemnly complained, 'There's nowhere to put anything.' And there wasn't: suddenly relieved of the necessity to put everything away, we had put nothing away. And although matters have since improved to the stage where the mess at least gets heaped into piles, we clearly

have a long way to go.

In the same way, we are still childishly delighted by those everyday luxuries we once took for granted – like finding a chair beside the telephone instead of having to stand in draughty phone boxes... or stepping out of a hot bath into a towel warmed on a radiator... even being able to get out of both sides of the bed...

I mentioned all this to a former neighbour during one of my increasingly nostalgic walks down to the quay. He was ostentatiously filling his water tanks. He called me a landlub-ber and flung out his hand to encompass the view we have now sadly lost. He also grinned in an uncomfortably smug fashion when I nodded towards his hose and mentioned the shock of rediscovering water rates.

And standing there, looking at the twin impressions of *Lottie*'s keels still glaring up from the mud, I wondered if I had indeed sold out. Is a utility room with a washing machine or an armchair by an open fire really so important?

Anyway all this will come to an end in the spring when the boat goes back in the water and the tenancy agreement runs out. Then the only problem will be moving back aboard. We have already promised ourselves we shall be taking with us the merest fraction of what came off the boat, not to mention spending a week stowing it as we go.

Yet I for one will be glad to be afloat again. The Heavenly Twins may be compact and not over-generous when it comes to headroom but at least I won't go around cracking my skull on 300-year-old oak beams.

Busy Going Nowhere

Nobody mentions the cheap wine and sunshine, or waters so clear that you can see your anchor in 15 metres. Or, come to that, Monday mornings when the only urgency about getting up is in order to be at the fish market before they run out of baby calamari.

But you can thank Chay Blyth for that. He filled the oceans of the world with people Pushing Themselves to the Limit and feeling short-changed on their £18,750 if they failed to get a faceful of freezing spray every day before breakfast.

Suddenly the tricky business of explaining the liveaboard lifestyle to non-sailing friends acquired a whole new complexity. For instance someone who knew only that I lived on a boat asked brightly the other day, 'And did you sail around the world?' as if it were some sort of holiday destination.

The books never dwell on this aspect of the business. They tend to be big on cover pictures of trim white ketches anchored off palm-fringed beaches and carry plenty of advice about keeping cockroaches at bay; but nobody ever warns, 'Do not try to explain your plans to non-sailing friends.'

For despite the fact that the liveaboard population is increasing at the sort of rate that sometimes makes one wonder whether there will be enough palm-fringed beaches to go round, there are still an awful lot of people who view the idea of life without a double garage in the same terms as life on the moon. And is it any wonder, when their entire understanding of sailing comes from sitting over Sunday breakfast reading about gung-ho tyros losing masts down among the icebergs?

It is time somebody wrote about the other record for sailing round the world. I understand it is 18 years but since the holders are somewhat laid back about great achievements, you never get to hear much about them. But the fact is that most long-term cruising boats spend about 95 per cent of their time in harbour.

This is one of the first surprises, and more of a surprise, considering that the new life begins with the rush to sell the house and distribute the heirlooms around the rest of the family and argue about why the holding tank won't fit. No wonder it is so hard to come to terms with a pace of life that is ultimately so slow that sometimes it shows no sign of movement at all.

One of the best pieces of advice anyone gave us was not to go anywhere at all for six months but just to sit on the boat and acclimatise to the idea of not having to go any-where.

Besides, it would take that long to trace the leak in the water tank and find out why the heater kept going off and where we put the passports.

Then there was the matter of clothes. We gave great thought to this and even went out and bought what some-times seemed like a whole new wardrobe, reasoning that once we stopped work we would be shopping at Oxfam. And what happened? Most of the new wardrobe ended up at Oxfam. I am proud to say that after a single summer of this new life I recovered the waistline I vaguely remember from 25 years ago. Of course some people go the other way – but the message is the same – that nothing stays the same.

And that goes for every aspect of life - as they will tell you down at Torrevieja Marina in Spain. Readers of the Heavenly Twins Owners Association newsletter have been enthralled by the tale of the couple who retired onto their boat only to find that the wife would rather have retired onto another gentleman's boat.

However, being the understanding type, she arranged for a replacement – another sailing wife who had found her skipper did not improve with age either. Happily she was also moored in Torrevieja.

Apparently this game of matrimonial musical chairs was played out in the space of a single day, with a good deal of baggage being carted up and down the pontoons and an astonishing amount of whispering in the showers. The locals wondered why nobody got stabbed.

Best of all, one of the new couples then decided the cruis-ing life was not for them after all, and so the others were able to buy their generator and trailing log.

That any of the parties should admit to this at all – let alone write a cheery account of it along with advice on the Spanish Navtex service – demonstrates just how different things are on the other side of the rather complicated change--of-address notice which still fails to explain the exact function of Ship-to-Shore.

Of course the Global Challenge types would say that nothing is ever the same again for them either. But for the most part they are going back to life ashore. They will have conquered their Everest and returned.

Those of us living here in the foothills simply nod with bemused interest as they whizz past.